To Appomattox and Beyond

TO APPOMATTOX AND BEYOND

*The Civil War Soldier in
War and Peace*

Larry M. Logue

The American Ways Series

IVAN R. DEE   *Chicago*

Library of Congress Cataloging-in-Publication Data:
Logue, Larry M., 1947–
    To Appomattox and beyond : the Civil War soldier in war and peace
/ Larry M. Logue.
      p. cm. — (The American ways series)
    Includes bibliographical references and index.
    ISBN 1-56663-093-2 (alk. paper). —ISBN 1-56663-094-0 (pbk. :
alk. paper)
    1. United States. Army—History—Civil War, 1861–1865.
2. Confederate States of America. Army—History. 3. United
States—History—Civil War, 1861–1865—Social aspects. 4. United
States—History—Civil War, 1861–1865—Veterans. I. Title. II. Series.
E492.3.L64 1996
973.7'42—dc20   95-30217

For Barbara

Contents

Preface

THIS BOOK SHIFTS the perspective on the Civil War and its aftermath from generals and politicians to the ordinary soldier. The literature on rank-and-file Rebels and Yankees has grown in recent years, and we can begin to take stock of their later lives as well as their wartime experience. Three million men served in the war, a larger share of the population than in any other American conflict, and more than 600,000 died, likewise the most in our history. The horror and exhilaration of combat affected everyone involved, and echoed throughout their lives. The sheer numbers of Civil War veterans ensured that their needs and convictions would carry special weight.

Mutual animosity between North and South had been smoldering for decades before the fighting, but two events caused resentment to flare into open conflict. In October 1859 the antislavery activist John Brown and twenty-two followers seized the federal arsenal at Harpers Ferry, in what is now West Virginia. Brown had hoped to touch off a widespread slave revolt, but federal troops and local militiamen quickly retook the arsenal and captured Brown and six surviving supporters. All were tried and hanged within a few months, but shock waves from the incident lasted much longer. Many Southerners believed that the Northern subversion they had long feared was now at hand, and they lashed out at potential threats. Southern governments stockpiled weapons and revived dormant militia companies; Southern citizens assaulted some Northern-born neighbors and sent others fleeing for their lives.

The final spark came in the fall of 1860. By then, political parties could no longer bridge sectional differences; the Democrats, the one remaining national party, had split apart in the summer over federal policy on slavery. Northern Democrats nominated Stephen A. Douglas for president, while Southern Democrats chose the current vice-president, John C. Breckinridge. Abraham Lincoln was the Republican nominee, and a group of older politicians who still hoped to avoid disunion formed the Constitutional Union party and nominated John Bell for president. With the Democrats' North-South coalition gone, Lincoln received enough votes to win the election, but the result signaled the final breach in the Union—Lincoln carried every free state but no slave states. Convinced they would be powerless against a hostile government if they remained in the Union, Southern "fire-eaters" demanded secession. South Carolina withdrew on December 20, 1860, and by February 1 six other states had followed suit. Before month's end the seven states had formed the Confederate States of America, with its capital in Montgomery, Alabama, and Jefferson Davis as president.

All this happened before Abraham Lincoln took office; Democrat James Buchanan was president until March 4, 1861. Believing he had no authority to use force to prevent secession, Buchanan hoped that a last-minute compromise might somehow emerge. None did, and the newly inaugurated Lincoln inherited a critical situation at Fort Sumter in South Carolina. The fort's federal garrison was caught between a dwindling stock of supplies and the Confederate artillery of Charleston harbor. When Lincoln announced his intention to resupply the fort, Davis gave the order to fire, and the Union garrison surrendered on April 14, 1861. In response to the attack, Lincoln called for 75,000 militiamen and ordered a blockade of Southern ports, acts that Southerners in turn took to be a declaration of war. Virginia, Arkansas, Tennessee, and North Carolina cast their lot with the seceded states, and the enlarged Confederacy moved its capital to Richmond, Virginia.

Both sides organized armies remarkably quickly, and the first major battle took place at Bull Run, Virginia (known to Southerners as Manassas) on July 21, 1861. The Confederates routed the overconfident Yankees, making it clear the war would be long and costly. Indeed, for nearly two years the armies fought to an appallingly bloody stalemate. The Union's plan to take control of the Mississippi River proceeded steadily, if slowly, under General Ulysses S. Grant, but the early campaign to capture Richmond was a failure. George B. McClellan brought a large army close to Richmond in the spring of 1862, only to be driven back with sharp counterattacks by General Robert E. Lee. In September, Lee's own foray into Union territory was turned back at Antietam, Maryland, in a battle that killed six thousand men in one day. Lincoln used the modest Union success as a pretext for announcing his plans to issue an Emancipation Proclamation, declaring that all slaves in Confederate territory on January 1, 1863, would be free.

The military deadlock continued: after their success at Antietam, Union forces were badly beaten at Fredericksburg and Chancellorsville, Virginia, in December 1862 and May 1863 (though in the latter battle the Confederates lost a revered commander, General Thomas "Stonewall" Jackson). But decisive events were around the corner. In the West, Grant captured the vital Confederate stronghold at Vicksburg, Mississippi, on July 4, 1863, and the Mississippi River was soon in Union hands. In the East, Lee attempted another invasion of the North but was defeated at Gettysburg, Pennsylvania, beginning his retreat on the day that Vicksburg fell. Much hard fighting remained, but now the North had the upper hand.

In early 1864 Grant became general-in-chief of all Union armies and took command of the assault on Richmond; he assigned William Tecumseh Sherman to overcome Confederate resistance to the south and west. While Grant attacked Lee in Virginia, Sherman closed in on Atlanta; news of his capture of the city in September helped Lincoln win reelection two months later (against George McClellan). Sherman and his army then set out on their "march to the sea," an expedition meant·to break Southerners' spirit by laying waste to the countryside. In December 1864 Sherman's men reached Savannah, having cut a swath of destruction through Georgia; they then turned toward South Carolina to continue the job.

Meanwhile, Grant was tightening the noose around Lee's Army of Northern Virginia. Attacking, pulling back and moving southward, and then attacking again, Union forces wore down a Confederate army already decimated by casualties, hunger, and desertion. Confederate officials abandoned Richmond in early April 1865, and Lee surrendered at Appomattox Court House on April 9. Confederate armies elsewhere would follow suit in the weeks ahead, but the war was to take yet another key casualty: on April 14 Confederate partisan John Wilkes Booth shot and fatally wounded Abraham Lincoln.

It appeared at first that Lincoln's successor, Andrew Johnson, would favor harsh treatment of ex-Confederates. Soon, however, Johnson made clear his support for restoration of Southern white supremacy, putting him on a collision course with congressional Republicans. From 1866 to 1868 Johnson and Congress fought over Reconstruction: Congress enacted guarantees of civil rights for Southern freedpeople, Johnson vetoed them, and Congress overrode his vetoes. In 1868 the House of Representatives impeached Johnson and the Senate came within one vote of convicting him; the remainder of Johnson's term saw a truce in the fighting, and his successor, Ulysses S. Grant, was a Republican who was less at odds with Congress.

By 1870 the former Confederate states had met Congress's requirements for ensuring freedpeople's rights and had been readmitted to the Union, but conservative Southern whites would not tolerate the Republican-dominated state governments. In state after state, exploiting Republican weaknesses where they could and using violence elsewhere, Democrats overthrew Republican rule. Congressional Republicans had less interest in and control over Reconstruction than in the 1860s; an economic depression beginning in 1873 and scandals in Grant's administration occupied national politics, and the Republicans lost control of the House of Representatives in the 1874 election. As part of the compromise that resolved the disputed 1876 presidential election, the new president, Republican Rutherford B. Hayes, removed federal troops from South Carolina and Louisiana in 1877. Reconstruction ended with the quick fall of these last Southern Republican governments.

Until the final years of the nineteenth century, there were no more wars to distract Americans from the memory of the Civil War. In April 1898, amid a public outcry over Spain's treatment of its Cuban subjects and following the suspicious explosion of the American battleship *Maine* in Havana's harbor, the United States declared war on Spain. The war lasted less than four months and produced fewer than four hundred battle deaths before an overmatched Spain surrendered. The United States inherited control of Cuba and ownership of the Philippines and other distant possessions; Americans increasingly turned their gaze outward, away from the sectional conflict of an earlier era.

These central events shaped the experience of those who fought in the Civil War. Who they were and how they responded to the developments of their era will be explored in the chapters to follow.

To Appomattox and Beyond

1

Raising an Army in the North

NORTHERN SOCIETY WAS rapidly changing on the eve of the Civil War, and some of these changes affected the way Northern men would view military service. One clear sign of change was the extraordinary rise of Northern cities. The nation as a whole was growing—each decade from 1790 onward, the American population increased by about one-third, the fastest growth rate in the world. But cities were growing much faster. The population of New York, the nation's largest city, rose by nearly 70 percent in the 1850s, surpassing a million; Philadelphia, the next largest city, grew by 39 percent to more than a half-million.

Some newer cities exceeded even these rates. Buffalo, which had only 8,000 people in 1830, grew to more than 80,000 by 1860, and Newark, New Jersey, which had not existed as a town in 1830, passed 70,000 just thirty years later. The most remarkable increase occurred in Chicago, which went from a few cabins in 1830 to more than 100,000 people in 1860. Smaller cities and towns likewise flourished throughout the North. The South had New Orleans, whose growth was similar to that of Northern cities, but only one in ten Southerners lived in cities and towns on the eve of the Civil War, compared with more than a third of people in New England and the Mid-Atlantic states.

Just as they always had, most Americans still lived on farms and in the villages that served them, but farming could no longer provide a living for everyone in a population that doubled every twenty-five years. The adventurous could still find farm land to the west, but cities, especially Northern cities, were the great magnets of opportunity. Antebellum cities were built on commerce: the nation's population passed 30 million in the 1850s, and feeding, clothing, and otherwise supplying this many people created an immense flow of goods through cities like Buffalo and Philadelphia, with money to be made at every step. The cities also had manufacturing, though not yet an industrial revolution. Large, mechanized factories employing armies of workers were found primarily in the textile industry; most other manufacturing took place in small shops where a master craftsman or merchant watched over a few workers. But here too there was money to be made for people willing to put up with the overcrowding, crime, and appalling death rates that plagued the cities.

And on they came, young people leaving the countryside to become bank clerks or dockworkers or shoemakers, immigrants coming from western Europe to become weavers or day laborers, and African Americans fleeing the South to become porters or domestic servants. Yet cities did not bring prosperity to all newcomers. Work that was plentiful and steady in good times could become sporadic in a slow season and disappear in a depression. On the eve of the Civil War the North had just emerged from one such depression, touched off in 1857 by the failure of a major investment firm and the collapse of wheat prices. Merchants, bankers, and manufacturers cut back or closed down at times like these, and there was no unemployment insurance for clerks or ironworkers or anyone else whose wages ceased. Unpredictable bouts of un-employment were a hard fact of life for men and women in the North's commercial economy.

Another lesson had to be learned by those who wanted a living wage in the world of urban commerce. Rural Ameri-cans had taken for granted that people made most of their own decisions, within limits set by nature. Farmers decided what and when to plant, storekeepers decided what supplies to order, and success depended on providence and one's own industry. Likewise, tailors, blacksmiths, and other village arti-sans had controlled production in their shops. But working for wages involved an entirely different set of conditions. When an employer offered work, employees worked by the owner's rules. Employers decided the hours of work and the tasks to be done, and they owned the place of work and often the equipment the workers used. In exchange for wages, workers had to give up much of the control over life that they or their parents had enjoyed. Labor unions sometimes chal-lenged employers' worst abuses: workers demanded and won a ten-hour day in many industries, and twenty thousand Massachusetts shoemakers struck in 1860 to protest low wages. But unions faced bitter opposition from owners and public officials and were usually crippled by economic depres-sions. Most workers had to cope as individuals with the new rules of work.

Self-control was the approved method for individuals to deal with the demands of wage employment. Self-discipline was nothing new in antebellum America: the New England Puritans had preached against idleness and waste in the seven-teenth century, and Benjamin Franklin had promoted rigor-ous self-discipline in the eighteenth century. But the overwhelming emphasis on self-denial in the nineteenth cen-tury was unprecedented. Social reformers, educators, writers of guidebooks on child-rearing, and ministers pleaded with Americans to reject temptation, reminding them of the consequences of indulgence in sex, drinking, gambling, and idleness. Prominent men and women insisted that every act of self-indulgence broke down character as well as the body (in men, for example, every sex act drained away vital fluid), and would lead to crime or insanity.

Influenced by this conviction, officials of penitentiaries, insane asylums, and poorhouses tried to indoctrinate residents in self-discipline. Public officials insisted that poverty, for example, was "the result of such self-indulgence, unthrift, excess, or idleness, as is next of kin to criminality." School officials were similarly determined to teach "habits of regularity, punctuality, constancy and industry in the pursuits of business."

Parents in the growing middle class worked long and hard to inspire self-control in their children. Unlike farmers, most urban fathers spent the day away from the household, working for pay, and it became the mother's job to instill in sons and daughters a conscience for self-regulation. By doling out or withholding affection and approval, mothers (occasionally reinforced by their husbands) cultivated the "tyrannical monitor," as one nineteenth-century American called his conscience. Parents wanted a properly functioning conscience to be an internal brake on their children's impulses, to head off wrongdoing before it could begin. Parents and advice-givers agreed that only through self-control could people achieve happiness and success: everyone must religiously avoid wasting energy, money, and time. If people heeded this advice, they would have little trouble with the time and work demands of employers.

Was this approach successful? It was preached most urgently in the Northeast, and evidence from several Northeastern communities shows that premarital pregnancies declined in the nineteenth century, one hint that Americans accepted reformers' preaching on sexual restraint. Yet there are also indications of strong resistance to the dictates of self-control. Historian Anthony Rotundo argues that middle-class boys in the nineteenth century were strongly inclined to impulsive violence and vandalism; other evidence of resistance comes from strikes by workers, many of whom refused to embrace employers' definitions of self-discipline.

The North showed other signs of change before the Civil War. The outside world was coming ever closer, even for people who lived far from the cities. Telegraph lines stretched from coast to coast and into most communities, and railroad construction was booming. More than twenty thousand miles of rails were laid in the 1850s, bringing most Northerners within two days' travel of one another. Northern farmers had become more involved with the wider world and were now producing most of their wheat, corn, and livestock for sale; a few decades earlier, most crops raised outside the densely settled New England states had been for home use. And Northerners, like Americans in other regions, were a restless people. Young men and older families alike, especially when they had little land or other wealth, moved frequently from place to place in search of a better living. Historians studying nineteenth-century communities have found that as many as half the residents moved away each decade.

Yet many Northerners clung to old habits even as they did business with the outside world. Many rural and small-town families did not move about, and they were the core of neighborhoods of friends and relatives dependent on one another for farming help, church fellowship, and socializing. Farm women, even when their husbands raised crops for sale, continued to produce butter, eggs, and clothing for exchange and home use. When the crops were harvested and sold, men would often take their favorite rifle and hunting dogs and head to the woods, seeking game as had generations before them.

These men would also take up arms for their country. About 100,000 men had volunteered for the war against Mexico in the 1840s. Most of the soldiers had come from south and west of the Appalachians, but war fever had caught up communities everywhere. Most towns thus had at least a few Mexican War veterans who could entertain young people with their exploits in the most recent war.

But Americans distrusted regular armies, and they even refused to take militia duty seriously. Communities were supposed to ensure that their adult males were ready for emergency military duty, but militia responsibilities had become mainly a source for officers' titles and an excuse for getting, in the words of one observer, "supremely drunk" at periodic drills. As the sectional crisis deepened in the late 1850s and early 1860s, a number of states tried to revive their militia units.

Secession came quickly on the heels of Abraham Lincoln's election. South Carolina, where secessionist sentiment had been strong for years, voted to secede in December 1860, forcing its neighbors either to join it or risk having to take up arms against fellow Southerners. By February 1861 six states chose to join South Carolina. On April 15, the day after Fort Sumter fell to Confederate forces in South Carolina, Lincoln issued a call for 75,000 state militiamen. After four upper South states joined the seven that had already seceded, the President recognized that his call-up would scarcely produce an adequate army. On May 3 Lincoln asked for 60,000 additional volunteers for three years' service in the army and navy. Congress, meeting in July, authorized 500,000 more volunteers, and when Union troops were routed at Bull Run before the month was out, lawmakers called for another half-million troops. Mobilizing troops was still seen as a state and local responsibility, so federal officials assigned troop quotas to the states and counted on them to do the rest.

At first the states were largely successful. Governors called for smaller communities to raise companies (about one hundred men each) and larger areas to raise regiments (usually ten companies). Local patriotism then took over. Lawyers or merchants ran newspaper advertisements and printed posters such as this one from Massachusetts: "War! War! War! . . . All citizens are requested to meet at the town hall this evening to see what can be done." At such a rally a local band would play patriotic anthems; politicians, visiting dignitaries, and perhaps a Mexican War veteran would exhort the crowd to stand up for their state and their Union; and local men would come forward. The volunteers would elect their officers, who were often the organizers of the recruiting, and make ready to go to war. Local women would be busy too, making flags, collecting supplies, and even sewing uniforms in these days before the Union adopted standard-issue blue. Within a week or two the new company would be ready for its send-off. Again the brass bands would play, the women would formally present their flag to the troops, farewells would be said, and the soldiers would be on their way to be mustered into federal service. By early 1862, 700,000 troops were thus mobilized for the Union army, and the War Department began to close its recruiting offices.

But by the summer of 1862 it became clear that more soldiers would be needed and that they would be harder to recruit. The war was going well in the West: the army and navy had taken fifty thousand square miles of territory and had captured Memphis and New Orleans on the Mississippi River, though the formidable defenses of Vicksburg remained in

Confederate hands. But in the East the Union campaign to take Richmond had gone miserably. General George McClellan's Army of the Potomac, after advancing close enough in May to hear the Confederate capital's church bells, fell back under sharp attacks by what McClellan wrongly believed was a much larger Confederate army. By July the assault on Richmond was abandoned by a high command convinced that McClellan's failure of nerve had cost a chance for a quick end to the war.

But it was not strategic failures alone that alarmed federal officials. The human toll of Civil War battles was beginning to hit home: in the western Battle of Shiloh, 13,000 Union soldiers had been killed, wounded, or captured; in Virginia the Union lost 5,000 men at Seven Pines, and McClellan's army suffered 16,000 more casualties in the Seven Days' Battle that led to the Richmond campaign's abandonment. Thousands more died of disease, and it would not be easy mobilizing more troops among civilians who were well aware of these losses. Lincoln called for 300,000 more soldiers in July, but it was clear that the days of the patriotic rush to war were over.

To fill their quotas under this new call, state and local officials inflated the traditional payment of soldiers' bounties. Once meant primarily as a discharge payment, the bounty now became a bonus for enlistment. The federal government allowed only a $25 advance on its bounty, but state and local governments added amounts averaging about $100 to coax men into new volunteer companies. If this did not work, the federal government threatened to intervene. In July 1862 Congress ordered the states to activate their militia units (and empowered federal officials to do so if state leaders dragged their feet), and to draft enough militiamen to cover any shortfall in meeting troop quotas. Most states met their 1862 quotas with volunteers, but some had to resort to militia drafts. In several places where support for the war was lukewarm, mobs attacked and occasionally killed the militia's enrolling officers.

Yet African Americans, the one group eager to go to war with or without bonuses, remained unwelcome in the army. The eminent black spokesman Frederick Douglass condemned "the pride, the stupid prejudice and folly" that compelled Northerners "to fight only with your white hand, and allow your black hand to remain tied." But the prevailing mood among whites was expressed by a Pennsylvania soldier, who predicted that if blacks were allowed in the army "our own Soldiers will kill more of them than the Rebs would." As a result, the government's early policies on black troops were halting and contradictory.

But as casualties mounted and Northern morale worsened, the prospect of black troops taking up the burden of fighting became more appealing. Lincoln's preliminary Emancipation Proclamation in September 1862 endorsed a war to change Southern society, and the final version of the Proclamation on New Year's Day officially authorized African-American troops. Some black regiments had already been organized in the West, and one unit had seen action. Now, in 1863, recruiters began to enlist thousands of African Americans as Union soldiers.

But the need for men seemed endless. The mobilization crisis of 1862 repeated itself in the spring of 1863. Vicksburg still stood in the West, and Union forces had been badly beaten at Fredericksburg, Virginia, late in 1862. Worse still, the government had accepted some two-year recruits early in the war, and these troops were about to go home. As a result, Congress enacted a full-scale military draft in March 1863. Federal provost marshals were to visit congressional districts and identify men aged twenty to forty-five who had not joined the army. Their names were then to be drawn by lot to fill any shortfalls in their districts' volunteering.

Men subject to the draft did, however, enjoy some alternatives to service. They could still volunteer and avoid the stigma of being a conscript. Otherwise, to avoid joining the army, they could pay a $300 "commutation" fee that exempted them until the next draft (a provision which was largely repealed in 1864). Or they could hire a substitute, who would exempt them from future drafts as well. Fewer than 10 percent of the men whose names were drawn were in fact conscripted into the army; the rest volunteered, left for parts unknown, were exempted for medical reasons or as family providers, or bought their way out.

The draft, especially its exemptions for those who could afford them, dramatically intensified opposition to the war. Workers angrily protested in cities and towns from the Midwest to New England. In New York in 1863, Irish workers attacked draft officials and wealthy-looking men and then turned their fury on any African Americans they could find, seeing in them the cause of the war. The New York riot killed more than a hundred people and injured three hundred others. But the draft also had its intended effect on enlistments: although only 46,000 men were conscripted into the army, 800,000 others enlisted or reenlisted after the draft went into effect.

In all, nearly two million whites and almost 180,000 African Americans served in the Union army, or about 35 percent of the military-age population of the North. Who were they, and why did some join while others stayed away? The first answer to this question is *youth*. Studies of Northern enlistments have consistently shown that the highest rate of enlistment was among men in their late teens: 40 to 50 percent of them joined the army, whereas enlistment rates dropped to well under 20 percent among men over age thirty. Historian Reid Mitchell has argued that soldiering offered young men a definitive passage to manhood, which helps to explain the enthusiasm of young men early in the war. When word came of Fort Sumter's fall, James Snell, for example, "could not controll my own feelings . . . and would have shouldered my gun and started . . . had it not been for the earnest entreaty of my Parents." But this opportunity was bound up with patriotic duty for young soldiers. An Ohioan knew that he "would prove one of the most neglectful of sons" unless he risked his life for "the good form of government for which [his grandfather] gave seven years of the best of his life, [and] which has made me what I am." In this respect Union soldiers were like soldiers in most volunteer armies—young and eager to demonstrate their manly patriotism.

But we must remember that this war had a character of its own. James Snell's recollection of nearly losing control is an important clue to understanding Northern soldiers. The concern with self-control that was so prominent a feature of Northern society appears repeatedly in the writings of Union soldiers. They longed to achieve self-discipline: a Massachusetts soldier declared that a fallen comrade had been "absolutely cool and collected. . . . It is impossible for me to conceive of a man more perfectly master of himself." Inner discipline was also how Union soldiers defined themselves in contrast to others. A Union general believed that the war's cause was Southerners' "lawless and malignant passion," and soldiers often wrote of their need to punish the South's rebelliousness, to impose the discipline that Southerners had rejected. White men likewise contrasted themselves with black soldiers in their own army: where whites were supposed to be cool and controlled, one white officer believed that his black troops were "affectionate, enthusiastic, and dramatic beyond all others."

Other clues to understanding Union soldiers come from the characteristics of those who served and those who did not. Overall the Union army contained about the same percentage of farmers, skilled laborers, and other workers as did the adult male population, but aggregate comparisons overlook differences in age, property holding, and so on. Several studies comparing soldiers with noncombatants in Northern communities have found that Northerners' decisions were heavily influenced by their economic situation. When age is held constant, it becomes clear that, in areas where commerce predominated, artisans, unskilled laborers, and even white-collar men (and their sons) were more likely to serve than were farmers; where farming dominated, men with little or no property (and their sons) were especially likely to enlist.

There were, of course, individual and group exceptions to the enlistment findings. Oliver Wendell Holmes, Jr., who would later become a Supreme Court justice, and Robert Gould Shaw, son of a wealthy Boston family, served in Massachusetts regiments. And immigrants, especially the Irish, were less likely to enlist: some had not applied for citizenship and thus were not subject to the draft, and those who did serve often encountered hostility from native-born troops. But in general, Northerners with reason to worry about their livelihood—who depended on the whims of business cycles and employers or on small plots of land, sometimes owned by a landlord—were more likely to respond to the economic incentives offered by military service.

Did local politics also affect Northerners' enlistment decisions? It makes sense to suppose that, in communities that supported Lincoln's Republican party, loyal Republicans would eagerly join the army and insist that their neighbors do likewise, and that Democratic communities would discourage enlistment. Some studies have indeed found that draft evasion and desertion were more frequent in places with lukewarm support for the war, and their Democratic sympathies may have contributed to immigrants' reluctance to enlist. But a study of two New Hampshire towns has shown that men in the Democratic town were *more* likely to enlist than those in the Republican town. Local political climates thus appear to have been a less consistent influence on Northern men's enlistment decisions than was concern for their livelihood.

The monetary incentives for enlistment became impressive as the need for men became more urgent. In 1863 the federal government raised its enlistment bounty to $300; together with state and local bounties, volunteers could easily receive much more than the $460 yearly earnings of an average worker. With more modest bonuses already in effect for some time, and with payments for enlisting plus provisions for buying one's way out of service, it is clear that recruitment acted as an economic market for most of the war.

The importance of this market is demonstrated by the treatment of African-American soldiers. Primarily to make black troops more acceptable to hostile whites, the army refused to allow African Americans to participate as equals in the recruitment market. Blacks often received less bounty money than did whites, and recruiters sometimes refused to pay black soldiers the bounties they were owed. Moreover, until late in the war, blacks received half or less, depending on rank, of whites' monthly pay. Nonetheless, 38,000 blacks from the free states enlisted, and 140,000 Southern blacks defied white Southerners' harassment and threats to their families and joined the Union army.

Again largely to make black troops palatable, Union officials decided that black regiments should have white officers and took special care in selecting them. Convinced that black men needed extraordinary leadership to make them into adequate soldiers, and aware that black units would face hostility, army officials created special examining boards for black units' officers. The War Department had largely replaced officer elections with examinations in white units as well, but candidates for black units received exceptional grilling on army procedures and general knowledge. Forty percent of candidates failed the test, and the failure rate would have been higher except for a special school created to prepare candidates for the test. The poor quality of officers, which often crippled the effectiveness of white units, was undoubtedly a lesser problem among the United States Colored Troops.

A wide assortment of men joined the Union army, but there were patterns we can identify among them. Those who fought for the Union tended to be young, to be (or to have a parent who was) in an occupation with an uncertain future, and to be concerned with self-control. How did military service meet the needs of such men? A few soldiers frankly admitted that economic insecurity drove them to enlist. Historian David Blight, examining the career of Charles Brewster, has argued that enlistment in a Massachusetts regiment was Brewster's "effort to compensate for prior failure" as a store clerk "and to imagine a new career." Other soldiers, however, spoke of patriotism and duty in referring to their enlistment. Some historians have concluded from such sentiments that wage earners, needing opportunities in a commercial, free-labor society, gladly fought against a South they saw as an aristocratic, slavery-bound threat to their livelihood. But in rural areas, small farmers were the men most likely to enlist, and most cared little about jobs for wage workers.

Military-age men probably thought as much about what they had to *sacrifice* as what they had to *gain* by going to war. If he enlisted, a master shoemaker who had been put out of business by shoe factories was not giving up the same security as was a prosperous wheat farmer. Henry Bear of Illinois was explicit about this kind of reasoning: "I studied the cost and measured the way before I enlisted." As bounties surpassed $400 or $500, the economic sacrifice lessened, and more financially secure men could be induced into the army. But the backbone of the Union army were men for whom the dangers of war were not a bad trade for a tenuous future in a shop or on the farm.

Perhaps the most famous cliché to emerge from the Civil War is the accusation that this was "a rich man's war and a poor man's fight." Those making this charge against the Union army had an inkling of the truth, but it was not exactly the poor who predominated in the army; craftsmen and clerks were also common in the ranks. Union recruitment, with its bonuses and loopholes, opened an alternative to an insecure world of work. A cliché that has also come down to us is that the Civil War was a conflict of "brother against brother." Besides its literal meaning—there are innumerable cases of brothers fighting on opposite sides, from generals on down the ranks—does this phrase also tell a larger truth? Were the two armies essentially alike?

2

Mobilizing a Confederate Army

A UNION OFFICER voiced a common opinion about Confederates when he described them as conspirators "who plotted and labored for the overthrow of the Republic." He was partly right: for decades before the Civil War, Southern political leaders had struggled to ensure that the federal government would protect what they saw as their right to property, including slaves, and to an orderly society. But Southerners vehemently denied that they staged a rebellion. In their view they were merely reacting to a chain of events that threatened to produce a Northern tyranny and lead to the destruction of Southern society. Using the federal power to hand out offices and other favors, Lincoln's Republicans would curry favor with the border states and upper South where slavery was weakest. Winning over state after state, Republicans would finally control enough states to end slavery by constitutional amendment. Secession, fire-eaters insisted, was no more a rebellion than was the revolution of 1776, when Americans likewise severed ties with a government that threatened their liberties.

Nevertheless, Southerners were far from unified. The South, from the Mason-Dixon line to Texas, was dominated by farming. Agriculture was at the heart of nearly every local economy, and even Southern cities were largely collection points for cash crops. But farming divided rather than united Southerners. A minority of Southerners, most numerous near the Atlantic seaboard and in the deep South, made their living by raising crops for sale—tobacco in tidewater Virginia and North Carolina, rice along the South Carolina and Georgia coasts, cotton in the lowlands from Georgia to Texas, and sugar in Louisiana. Most cash crops were labor-intensive, and most of the laborers were slaves. Owners of large numbers of slaves called themselves planters and formed the local elite. They traveled to Southern cities for business and to the North and Europe for pleasure, sent their sons to college, kept order in their communities, and held political offices.

But moving away from the plantation belts, one would find less and less of this income-producing agriculture. Landholdings and slaveholdings became smaller in Southern uplands and piney woods; typical farms might be eighty or ninety acres with a few slaves rather than the thousand or more acres and dozens of slaves on some "black-belt" places. Many upland families owned no slaves, and an increasing number did not own the land they farmed. Small farmers might put in a patch of cotton or tobacco where possible, but their first priority was sustenance. Upland farmers typically concentrated on corn, wheat, and livestock, using the labor of husband, wife, and children, and nonslaveholders might hire a few slaves or white farmhands. In addition, wives produced butter, eggs, and clothing to use or to exchange with neighbors.

Farther still from the plantation belts were the Southern mountain communities. The Appalachians and their foothills cut through the western parts of Virginia, the Carolinas, and Georgia, and the eastern parts of Kentucky and Tennessee. Mountain folk rarely saw a slave; most mountaineers lived in isolated settlements, raising their crops in valleys and hollows.

Lowlanders despised these mountaineers, and they returned the favor. Plantation elites, central governments, and the wars they made were alien to mountain people.

Yet the South's various classes of farmers coexisted. To be sure, there were class tensions in the antebellum South. Planters' contempt extended beyond mountaineers to include their own poorer neighbors, while plain folks' resentment of this disdain could flare into violence: an arrogant planter might have a barn burned or a slave murdered by a resentful neighbor. Though set after the war, William Faulkner's story "Barn Burning" illustrates a long tradition of common whites' resentment. In it a sharecropper, jealous of his "wolflike independence," twice strikes back at wealthy landlords' contempt by burning their barns.

But these tensions were usually kept in check by common interests. Small farmers could ordinarily count on wealthy neighbors for cotton ginning or the loan of a slave or two at busy times. Planters in turn needed commoners' votes for public office. And perhaps above all, planters upheld an ordered society. Planters were always on the lookout for signs of an uprising among their slaves or a threat to community order. The signs might be distinct—a stranger seen talking to slaves—or more indirect—gamblers or liquor-sellers moving into a town, for example. When they saw danger, planters moved quickly, often without benefit of the law. They would typically organize a vigilance committee, investigate the threat, and punish offenders with banishment, whipping, or hanging. Planters' vigilance made it clear that disobedience and dissent were not tolerated in their communities.

Punishing deviance obviously aided slaveholders, but it benefited nonslaveholders as well. It helped them in the present: reminders of slaves' subjugation encouraged even the poorest whites to feel superior to blacks, and affirming obedience assisted white men in maintaining authority over their wives, who were expected to obey husbands in much the same way as slaves did masters. And planters' rule promised to benefit nonslaveholders in the future: hard work and a few good harvests might enable a small farmer to buy a slave or two and thereby to benefit from the rigidly maintained slave system. In exchange for a few considerations such as voting, helping to build roads, and serving on juries, planters would thus combat all threats to white men's chance to farm their land and rule over their families as their forefathers had done.

As a result, planters could portray themselves as guardians of the Southern way of life, a way that was deeply rooted in personal relationships and tradition. Southern diaries and letters are filled with exchanges of visits lasting for weeks, trips to town for medicine for ailing neighbors, and deathbed vigils for fellow church members. Southerners tolerated only the slightest governmental regulation of their daily lives, but they eagerly embraced the intricate obligations of kinship and friendship. Providing money and hospitality to relatives honored one's heritage, reaffirming "the old fierce pull of blood," as Faulkner put it. Favors to and from friends affirmed the importance of judgments about character as a key to social life. Private responsibilities were as central to Southern life as public responsibilities were marginal, and Southerners had little use for distant governments or the reformers who dispensed advice to Northerners.

Men found this social world filled with challenges to their manhood. Status and reputation were paramount among Southern men, who never tired of competing at gambling, hunting, and drinking to establish a manly reputation. But a hard-won reputation could be ruined with one unanswered insult, and men had to be ready to respond with a challenge to a fight or a duel. Fistfights and knife fights between poorer

Southerners and duels within the gentry allowed men to defend (and for victors, to enhance) their manhood. Despite the efforts of state legislators and reformers who insisted that dueling was "the product of a barbarous age," the resort to violence was difficult to resist for young men obsessed with masculinity and honor.

Masculinity could also be demonstrated in military service. Southerners had made up a large part of the Mexican War army, but the peacetime United States army, amounting to about sixteen thousand troops stationed at remote western outposts, offered few opportunities for military distinction. Southerners had long been as lackadaisical about militia service as were Northerners, although Southern militia training became more spirited after Virginia and Maryland militiamen helped to put down John Brown's raid on Harpers Ferry in 1859.

Secession spurred still more military preparations, and the new Confederate Congress called for 100,000 one-year troops in March 1861. Volunteers overwhelmed local organizers, and new companies applied for arms and equipment faster than state governments could supply them. Following the capture of Fort Sumter, the Congress authorized 400,000 more soldiers (who could enlist for three years in exchange for government equipment, or for a year if they equipped themselves); by August the Confederacy had about 200,000 men under arms.

Mobilization proceeded in much the same way as in the North, but if anything Southern emotions were even more fevered. For one thing, Southern leaders expected an invasion, and they vigorously encouraged a sense of urgency in resisting a Northern assault. A Mississippian warned against "the tide of Northern fanaticism that threatens to roll through the South," and a newspaper spelled out the consequences if the invaders were to win: Southerners would lose their government, their slaves, and their right to vote, suffering "the grossest humiliation, to break down the stubborn pride and manliness native to the Southern breast."

The need to neutralize Unionism also intensified Confederate recruiting. Unionism was a complicated sentiment. Not surprisingly, many people in the Southern mountains, convinced that their states were governed by "bombastic, high falutin, aristocratic fools," as one North Carolinian put it, remained loyal to the Union. But some of the South's most prosperous slaveholders, especially cotton planters along the Mississippi River, were also skeptical of the cost of secession. Secessionists eventually prevailed in eleven slave states (Delaware, Kentucky, Maryland, and Missouri remained in the Union), and then built on their victory to overcome opposition to enlistment in the new army. Confederate recruiters found a hostile reception among mountain folk, who often sent a large number of soldiers to the Union; elsewhere, by staging torchlight processions, holding rallies, and banishing and otherwise intimidating Unionists, Confederate supporters did their best to subdue dissent and inspire an enlistment fever.

Women were also instrumental in persuading Southerners to enlist. While Northern women encouraged and supplied Union troops, young women in the South were especially insistent that men join the army. Southerners' exceptional concern about manhood bred insecurity, which in turn made men vulnerable to taunting, especially by women. Women had little genuine power in Southern society, but they were protected (outside the household, at least) from violent retaliation for insults. Women's demands and criticism, especially when aimed at would-be suitors, thus became standards of manhood. In Arkansas the future African explorer Henry Stanley, uncertain about the army, received a petticoat in the mail from a young woman; in Richmond it was said that the "ladies are postponing all engagements until their lovers have fought the Yankees"; and in Mississippi a woman challenged noncombatants to "be men once more, and make every woman in the land proud of having you as protectors."

All these forms of prodding, plus the excitement generated by success at Manassas (the Confederate name for Bull Run) in July 1861, produced thousands of companies for the Confederate army before the year was out. But Union forces scored key victories in the West during the winter, and General McClellan's army threatened Richmond in early 1862. The Confederate government now faced a manpower crisis: about half the troops in the field had enlisted for a year, and their terms would soon begin expiring. In April, faced with few choices, the Confederate Congress enacted the first national draft in America. The new law extended the term of the one-year men to three years, and required most other men aged eighteen to thirty-five to serve for three years. Exemptions were available for Confederate and state officials, for men in certain occupations such as railroad worker, telegraph operator, clergyman, or teacher—and for those who could hire a substitute.

Not surprisingly, the law was greeted with dismay among a populace that detested coercion. The words "usurpation" and "despotism" occasionally appear in the reactions of soldiers and politicians alike. The recollection of a Tennessee soldier is especially telling: after the draft took effect, he wrote, "a soldier was simply a machine, a conscript." To him and many of his comrades, the draft stripped military service of its distinction as an act of honor. Other Southerners, however, believed that the volunteer army had allowed too many men to stay at home, so that coercion was perfectly acceptable. "Good for conscription," wrote a newspaper editor, and a Mississippi soldier agreed that conscription "will pull a goodly number of [men] from around the fireplaces."

Like the Northern draft, Southern conscription filled the ranks. Relatively few Southerners were actually drafted into the Confederate army, but large numbers of men volunteered or hired a substitute. In 1862 the army showed a net gain (even after casualties) of 200,000 men. Still, in the long run the draft's inequities harmed the Confederate cause. Congress abolished substitution at the end of 1863 amid reports of widespread abuse, but lawmakers had already made another change that provoked fresh outrage. Responding to stories of plantations whose owners and overseers had left families unguarded against the supposed threat of slave attacks, Congress exempted from the draft one white man on each plantation with at least twenty slaves. Only a few thousand men took advantage of this exemption, but its class favoritism further aggravated soldiers' anger. James Skelton's resentment of planters who were "living at home enjoying life because they have a few negroes" was a typical reaction, while his brother expressed a grimmer assessment: "They intend to kill all the poor men." The twenty-slave exemption, which was eventually reduced to fifteen slaves but not eliminated, drove the wedge deeper between soldiers and the home front.

In all, about 900,000 men served as Confederate soldiers, or about 60 percent of those eligible (the draft eventually included men aged seventeen to fifty). Why did some Southerners join while others did not? When they explained their reasons for enlisting, Confederates described a patriotism that was often interchangeable with that of Union soldiers. One Confederate officer, for example, cited the need to "maintain inviolate the principles and rights of the Constitution," and another declared that he was preserving "Republican government in America." Since they expected the war to be fought on Southern soil, many Confederates added that they had joined the army in order to protect their homes and families. A Virginia soldier asserted that he was "defending what any man holds dear—his home and his fireside," and a Mississippian made a list of his motivations: he was fighting "for my wife & child & relatives and friends & country."

One historian found that the majority of soldiers on both sides made some mention of patriotic reasons for enlisting, and two-fifths had a political motivation such as states' rights or protecting the Union. Home defense as a motive was, of course, much more common among Confederates. But another study of Civil War letters and diaries concluded that personal concerns outweighed Southerners' references to duty. Two-thirds of Confederates made more allusions to personal glory, excitement, and the end of their enlistment than they did to patriotism or political ideals. And Union soldiers were not much different—most of them had at least as many references to personal concerns as to their duty.

Cultural historian Michael Barton's examination of the writings of men in both Civil War armies reveals that they held the same central values. Soldiers' most frequently mentioned concern was morality, followed by other personal values such as religious devotion and patriotism; political principles such as freedom and individualism were mentioned far less often. But though they *ranked* their values similarly, the two sides' *attachment* to them differed. Northern enlisted men were more concerned with self-restraint than with expressing emotions or evaluating character. Coming from a society in which self-control was ceaselessly prescribed as the key to achievement, Yankees tended to keep straightforward records of events; Southern soldiers, coming from a society that prized character and reputation, devoted much more of their letters and diaries to evaluating the kindness, bravery, and morality of those around them.

Southerners even wrote more condolence letters to their comrades' next-of-kin, for these letters were the ideal means of expressing admiration for a soldier's character. Where a typical condolence letter on the Union side commended a soldier as "cool and collected," a letter about Joseph F. Moseley of Mississippi focused on entirely different qualities. A comrade wrote that Moseley had "inspired Confidence, secured friends, that he 'grappled to his bosom with hooks of steel.' . . . His devotion to the cause of the South partook of that lofty enthusiasm which was chivalry itself."

There were highly visible exceptions to these tendencies. Robert E. Lee insisted that habits of self-control be instilled in his sons, and Stonewall Jackson was notorious for his relentless self-discipline. But these leaders were noteworthy for self-control *because* they stood out from their countrymen (and perhaps because they had attended the U.S. Military Academy at West Point). The self-control that many Northerners found essential had made only modest headway among Southerners.

Yet written testimony tells only part of the story. An important similarity between the characteristics of Southern and Northern soldiers was youth. Confederate enlistment rates could approach 80 percent among men in their late teens and twenties, but they fell steadily among older men. It made little difference whether young Southerners were single or married with families; the law, pressure from their neighbors, and their own enthusiasm brought them into the army.

But Southerners were unlikely to forget they were fighting a war to preserve their way of life, including the right to own slaves. Since slaveholders saw themselves as the special target of the Yankee invasion, and since slaveholders had always purged their communities of danger, they might be expected to be the likeliest candidates for participation in this war. Studies to date show that slaveholders (and their sons) did indeed take up their burden. In Mississippi, the greater the number of slaves held, the more likely a man was to enlist; similarly, in east Tennessee and tidewater North Carolina, slaveholders were more likely to become Confederates while smaller farmers and nonfarmers fought for the Union.

To underscore their belief in responsibility and in the unity of classes, a number of wealthy Southerners enlisted as foot soldiers: John Dooley, son of an affluent Richmond family, signed on as a private in the First Virginia Regiment, and Henry Clay Sharkey, a future member of Congress whose family owned more than fifty slaves, enlisted as a private in the Eighteenth Mississippi. (Even so, they kept some of the trappings of status—wealthy Confederates, including Private Sharkey, customarily brought along a slave or two as personal servants.) Despite the repeated condemnations of planters for their unwillingness to defend their own cause (they were "rusting in inglorious ease," according to one commentator), the evidence shows that planters and their sons did assume their usual role of eliminating a danger to their society.

With the intense legal and social pressures to join the Confederate army, how did more than a third of eligible men manage to avoid serving? Some obtained exemptions under the draft laws, but exempt men probably comprised less than 10 percent of the military-age population. Those who neither enlisted nor were exempted illustrate the tenuousness of Southern class cooperation. The war was another instance of the slaveholding gentry taking the lead in fighting a threat to the social order, but this time they first asked and then required other men to join them. Many Southerners refused from the start to follow the gentry's lead.

Militia rolls from several Mississippi counties show that between one-sixth and one-third of the military-age men who had lived there in the summer of 1860 were gone by the fall of 1861. Neither at home nor in the army, these men had left their county, probably for the West or the North. Before there was a draft, and while Confederates were still jubilant over their first major victories, a sizable number of men had already decided that the gentry's campaign was not for them. Some had had no choice: Southern communities drove away many Northern-born residents and outspoken Unionists as warfare approached. Other emigrants lived near the Mississippi River or the seacoast, and undoubtedly feared water-borne Yankee raiders; for still others, the demand that they leave their homes and join this crusade snapped their fragile ties to the gentry. Men who remained uncommitted during the war's early months would see their options narrow: Confederate officials eventually restricted travel, and enrolling officers combed the countryside to find eligible men for the army.

Union and Confederate soldiers thus shared some essential characteristics—primarily youth—and values—primarily a favoring of personal concerns over politics—but there were crucial differences in their motivations and attitudes. Northerners tended to enlist when their own circumstances offered little economic security, when army life was a fair exchange for a livelihood that might be eliminated by an employer or a landlord. Southerners, by contrast, were more likely to enlist if they already had economic security. Yankees threatened to take away their slaves, and though poorer Southerners enlisted at higher rates than poor Northerners joined the Union army, slaveholding was a special incentive to enlist in the Confederate army. Northern and Southern soldiers were also prepared to react differently to their experiences. Conditioned to exercise self-control, many Northerners would try throughout the war to restrain their emotions. Conditioned to express emotion in a world dominated by personal relationships, Southern soldiers would continue to dwell on their feelings and on the personal traits of friend and foe.

3

Union Troops Go to War

THE MEN WHO JOINED the Union army knew about death. Indeed, most would have witnessed at least one death in their own family. More than one-third of antebellum American children lost a brother or sister before reaching age fifteen, and an additional one-fourth saw a parent die. And death was rarely hidden away in some public institution. Particularly when the dying person was an adult, relatives and friends would gather around the deathbed in the hope of witnessing a "good death." Americans longed, as the author Herman Melville put it, "to expire mild-eyed in one's bed." When they did, observers were reassured both about the departed spirit and about their own fate.

But young men were seldom anxious about the prevalence of death. Youths did die in antebellum America: a young man might be killed in a train wreck, die in a brawl, or fall prey to an epidemic disease such as cholera. But his odds of dying were remote. Mortality estimates show that a twenty-year-old male in this period had better than a 90 percent chance of surviving until he was thirty. The young men who went to war were used to seeing deaths among children and the elderly but were unaccustomed to facing their own mortality.

Before they confronted death on the battlefield, however,

recruits faced other new experiences. Their journey from home took them to a "camp of instruction," where they were to become soldiers. Many of the recruits had never been this far from home, which made the experience novel enough, but enlisted men were also required to take orders and do menial chores. Habits of self-control inculcated in Northern society should have made following orders easy, but soldiers drew a distinction between serving in a people's army and working for an employer. One soldier pointed out that in the professional peacetime army, "officers follow the army for a business and the men for a living," but "in the volunteers we are all enlisted for a certain time and . . . I don't think it necessary to be so strict or exact." Most officers had no prior military experience; they were usually from the same community as their enlisted men, and, at least early in the war, they had been chosen by their men for the position. As a result, officers found they had to earn their soldiers' obedience rather than take it for granted. The Union officers most likely to gain respect were those who put the safety of their men first, as did George McClellan, those who dressed and acted as if they were no better than their men, as did Ulysses S. Grant and William T. Sherman, or those who demonstrated personal courage in battle, as did eleven-times-wounded Colonel Edward Cross. Officers who were arrogant or incompetent, on the other hand, quickly encountered various forms of retaliation. Soldiers had numerous ways of harassing unpopular officers, ranging from mocking orders to defecating in an officer's unoccupied tent to physical assault.

Having to do menial chores increased soldiers' resistance to orders. Most recruits had done chores as boys, but few expected that patriotic service would consist of endless rounds of gathering firewood, preparing food, digging latrines, and clearing brush. Marching drill took up a large part of soldiers' time in camp, and it was particularly tedious. Drill was meant to make some headway against recruits' resistance to discipline and to encourage teamwork, but soldiers hated it. "The first thing in the morning is drill, then drill, then drill again," wrote a soldier. "Then drill, a little more drill... Between drills, we drill and sometimes stop to eat a little and have roll-call." Even so, inexperienced officers often had reluctant men colliding with each other in formation and losing control of their horses in cavalry drills; supposedly attentive soldiers frequently burst into laughter at officers' attempts to give orders.

But camp life also provided plenty of reminders of soldiering's deadly side. Many recruits had brought their own rifles or shotguns, but the army supplied weapons as quickly as factories could turn them out and purchasing agents could buy them overseas. Union troops received a variety of firearms during the war, from smooth-bore muskets to breech-loading rifles, but the dominant weapon was the rifled musket. This was a muzzle-loader in which powder and bullet had to be driven down the barrel and a firing cap attached to the hammer before a shot could be fired. Although this process took seventeen steps, the grooves that spiraled down the inside of the barrel represented a technological advance over weapons used as recently as the Mexican War. The rifling allowed use of the famous "minié ball" (named for Claude Minié, one of its developers), which was actually a bullet with a hollowed-out base. When the gun was fired, the base expanded and gripped the grooves, and the bullet came out with a spin that made it much more accurate than the ball from a smooth-bore musket. In theory, the effective range of a rifled musket was nearly five hundred yards, versus less than one hundred yards for the smooth-bore.

Yet the guns were only as accurate as the soldiers firing them. Union troops got little target practice: officers were frequently as intimidated by musketry drill as were their men, especially since muskets could and did blow up in the faces of their users. And in an army this large, ammunition was often scarce, not to be wasted by shooting, as one unit did, at an effigy of Jefferson Davis. As a result, much of the small-arms fire of Civil War battles consisted of inaccurate fire from potentially accurate weapons, made worse by the pall of smoke that quickly obscured battlefields. Leander Stillwell of Illinois, for example, "was trying to peer under the smoke in order to get a sight of our enemies" at Shiloh, Tennessee, in 1862. When he told his lieutenant what he was doing, the officer screamed "shoot, shoot, anyhow." It is little wonder that a New York soldier reported seeing no more than one-third of shots hitting a stationary target in a rare target practice, or that historian Paddy Griffith estimates Union troops, firing under battle conditions, took two hundred shots for every one that hit an enemy soldier.

The war's most devastating killers appeared long before Union troops came under fire. Army camps brought together thousands of men in crowded and unsanitary conditions that were ideal for the spread of disease. Soon viruses and bacteria spread measles, smallpox, intestinal disease, and typhoid among the soldiers, and mosquitoes brought malaria; camp hospitals quickly filled, and physicians, who knew little about the cause of these diseases, were powerless against them. Soldiers died without ever seeing a battlefield, and regiments shrank in size. A soldier from Maine wrote that "though we enlisted to fight, bleed and die, nothing happened to us so serious as the measles." In the 125th Ohio and 12th Connecticut regiments, disease killed and disabled more than one-third of the original complement before either regiment fought a battle.

Recruits' prevailing attitude was disillusionment with these unexpected realities of the army, but soldiers also managed to shape camp life in ways that would last throughout the war. Long encampments were common, especially in the winter, and homesick soldiers tried to create a semblance of domestic life. Basic literacy was common among nineteenth-century Americans, and soldiers spent much of their time reading and writing. Their first priority was correspondence: men wrote letters under every conceivable condition, from first thing in the morning to lights-out at night to huddling on the battle-field, and they eagerly devoured responses from home. An observer estimated that a typical regiment sent 600 letters a day, and as many as 45,000 letters passed through Washington each day for the eastern armies. Soldiers read other material too, from newspapers to adventure stories in "dime novels" to the Bible and Charles Dickens. Some soldiers organized literary associations with their own lending libraries; a Massachusetts regiment early in the war maintained a library of more than five hundred books.

Most regiments had a chaplain who encouraged wholesome reading (and usually was the librarian) among his efforts at moral guidance. Chaplains held religious services, baptized converts, officiated at burials, visited the sick and wounded in the hospital, wrote and read letters for illiterate soldiers, and handled the mail. More broadly, religion offered guidelines for men away from parental supervision for the first time, and it promised God's protection for those fighting in a cause they believed was righteous. There were also occasional religious revivals in the Union army.

But as compared with the Confederate army, organized religion had only a limited impact on Union troops. Much of the problem was the chaplains' own shortcomings. Although many were conscientious, soldiers' comments suggest that a number were not up to the task. Chaplains received $100 a month—privates were paid $11 early in the war and $16 by the end—and a common assumption was that preachers "who can not make a good living at home, are the ones who strive to secure the position for the money." Soldiers' comments on sermons reveal some chaplains' inability to communicate with their troops. One chaplain "discussed *infant baptism* and closed with an earnest appeal, touchingly eloquent, to *mothers*," and another "preached doleful Sermons to the men about the hardships they will have to encounter, the Sickness & death and all the difficulties." Conscientious chaplains were equally critical of opportunistic colleagues. One chaplain complained that early in the war "men who were never clergy of any denomination" were appointed, and sometimes "the position was given to an irreligious layman." Historian Gerald Linderman has argued that chaplains' failings and the war's carnage, which came to seem increasingly random and senseless, caused many soldiers to doubt their early belief that the war represented the working of God's will.

If organized religion did not often meet soldiers' needs, music certainly did. Soldiers liked to listen to army brass bands, but they were positively obsessed with singing. They sang on the march, in camp, on the battlefield, and in the hospital; if Union and Confederate troops were within earshot, they might join together in a song. Patriotic morale-boosters such as "John Brown's Body" and "Battle Cry of Freedom" were highly popular among Union troops, but their real favorites were songs about home. "Home, Sweet Home" was probably the leading song on both sides, and so reflected soldiers' homesickness that bands were often forbidden to play it. But such expressions of longing could not be suppressed. Soldiers sang "My Old Kentucky Home," "When Johnny Comes Marching Home," and "When This Cruel War Is Over," the last of which sold a million copies of its lyrics. Songs allowed an expression of emotion appropriate to the moment, an expression that soldiers could control and that drew them together.

Since the army was the gateway to manhood for many of the recruits, they concentrated on activities that bridged the gap between boyhood and adulthood. Sports allowed soldiers to display their physical prowess, and they took part in individual competitions such as foot racing and boxing as well as organized sports, especially baseball. Indeed, the mingling of soldiers from different regions was instrumental in spreading baseball beyond its origins in the urban Northeast. In the winter, competitive urges were satisfied by organized snowball fights, distinguished from child's play by their roughness. These fights sometimes served as military exercises: officers might lead one regiment against another with bugles blaring and flags flying. Hard-thrown snowballs, sometimes containing stones, could and did cause injuries. In a battle between two New Hampshire regiments, a participant reported that "tents were wrecked, bones broken, eyes blacked, and teeth knocked out—all in *fun*."

Union soldiers were also caught between the youthful imperative to flout the rules of behavior and the mandate to exert manly self-control. Some, like Cyrus Boyd of Iowa, tried to cling to the ideals of self-discipline. Boyd condemned his comrades' eagerness "to abandon all their early teachings and to catch up with everything which seeks to debase," and he resolved to "keep the mind occupied with something new and keep *going all the time*." Other soldiers, however, viewed army life as an invitation to return to boyhood, and devoted themselves to seeing how far they could go in rule-breaking. Soldiers made an art of swearing—one private "wished the whole God damned Army and Navy and every other God damned thing was in hell"—and they were equally obsessed with gambling. Union troops played poker, a dice game called chuck-a-luck, and held cockfights, and would gamble anytime, anywhere. Witnesses told of poker hands that were completed under enemy fire, and soldiers were known to bet on the results of courts-martial for men caught gambling.

Practical joking allowed men to risk punishment and to embarrass unpopular soldiers. Pranks ranged from dumping water on a sleeping soldier to hazing new recruits to dangerous stunts such as mixing gunpowder with a soldier's pipe tobacco. But the masculine ritual that most exasperated authorities was drinking. Soldiers would drink any liquor they could get their hands on, from aged whiskey to the rawest "tanglefoot." Drunkenness triggered fights and caused injuries, and not only among enlisted men: an Illinois soldier noted one day that "Major Mellinger was so drunk that he fell off his horse." Frustrated commanders tried to cut off liquor supplies and punish drunkenness by tying offenders to a tree or making cavalrymen carry a saddle around the camp, and chaplains ceaselessly preached against the evils of drink. But liquor, in addition to its appeal as forbidden fruit, allowed soldiers some escape from the horrors of battle and the tedium of camp life. Soldiers' drinking and their resentment of those who tried to stop it appear to have increased during the war.

Soldiers thus viewed the camp as an exotic place where they could simultaneously take part in and escape from the dictates of manhood—but they also wanted it to be like home. Since most men in a company came from the same community, a soldier's companions were constant reminders of home, but a key feature of home life was missing—women. Soldiers occasionally saw women—female relatives visited regiments, and women nurses cared for soldiers in hospitals—but a typical complaint was that "I havent to say the real truth spoken three words to a femail sins I left home." One choice was to try an imitation: a number of regiments held dances with some of the men dressed as women. An Ohio soldier described a dance in which a comrade named Conway "has for a partner a soldier twice as big as himself whom he calls Susan. As they swing, Conway yells at the top of his voice: 'Come round, old gal!'"

Other soldiers were not interested in imitations. Some, especially if they had been well-to-do civilians, were received in nearby residences, even in the South. A soldier from Minnesota reported an evening spent in a planter's house, "conversing with the old gentleman's daughters & enjoying ourselves hugely. It is a long time since I was in a private house and as the 'gals' are quite sociable I enjoy the treat 'right smart.'" More often, soldiers went to prostitutes. Despite commanders' efforts (which once included dunking several prostitutes in the Mississippi River), prostitutes in camps and in nearby towns provided countless soldiers with "horizontal refreshments," to use the popular term. Venereal disease quickly appeared among the troops and became so serious that army officials in occupied Nashville opened a hospital for infected prostitutes in 1863. It is estimated that one in twelve Union soldiers contracted venereal disease during the Civil War.

Eventually camp life came to an end as new recruits prepared to go south for the first time or combat veterans broke camp for the next battle. The journey might begin by train or waterborne troop transport, but sooner or later troops would go on the march. Marching offered the excitement of impending battle, but it also made soldiers miserable. First-time marchers quickly discovered they were overloaded and would have to throw away cherished items from home, a process known as "simmering down." Some simmering-down had already occurred in camp, but now soldiers got down to the bare minimum. In the wake of marching soldiers lay discarded cavalry sabers, dress coats, books, and blankets. But marches were still a trial. They usually took place in the warm months, when southern heat and dust alternated with rain and mud. Marching was, of course, especially painful in ill-fitting shoes. A Connecticut soldier declared that "my gait was somewhat like that of a lame duck, but I waddled along . . . as fast as the remainder of our crew."

After the men finally arrived at the front, they began the ritual of preparation for battle. They received food rations and ammunition allotments, usually sixty paper cartridges containing powder and a bullet, plus a like number of firing caps. As the hour of battle approached and the troops took their assigned positions, the commanding officer would make a speech. These exhortations varied, but they were generally versions of this colonel's succinct instructions: "Now boys is the time to write your name. Let every man do his duty. Follow me!"

What happened next also varied widely. Sometimes Union troops would be ordered into a frontal assault on Confederate positions; on other occasions they would receive an assault behind fortified defenses; or they might exchange fire with enemy troops across a cornfield or in the woods. The assignment that soldiers feared most was the assault, in which they were called on to advance on the enemy's position in a series of lines, stopping several times to fire a volley of shots and reload, and then finish with a bayonet charge into the enemy lines. All too often, however, the outcome of an assault was a bloodbath. The Confederates had accuracy problems with their muskets (which were often captured from the Union), but they were nonetheless able to shoot down frightful numbers of attackers. Repeated assaults at Fredericksburg in 1862 resulted in nearly thirteen thousand Union dead and wounded among the Army of the Potomac, twice the Confederates' loss;

at Cold Harbor in 1864 the same army lost seven thousand men in a single assault, five times the enemy's casualties. Union assaults seldom overran Confederate defenses, and they produced a special horror among men who had been unaccustomed to seeing their age-mates die, much less be cut down in such numbers.

Soldiers likened an assault to charging through a storm of lead. One charging Yankee "thought it was raining bullets," and another leaned into the gunfire "the same as I would go through a storm of hail and wind." When an assault was over, whether or not it had routed the enemy, the aftermath was singularly terrifying. The faces of the dead after one battle looked "as if they had seen something that scared them to death." Another battlefield was so littered with corpses that wagons had run over them, leaving them "mangled and torn to pieces so that Even friends could not tell them." At Second Bull Run in Virginia, corpses lay "with their brains oozing out; some with their face shot off; others with their bowels protruding; others with shattered limbs." Soldiers filled their battle accounts with these graphic descriptions in an attempt to come to terms with the slaughter of their comrades.

Paddy Griffith argues that more reliance on double-time assaults, in which troops do not assist the enemy by stopping to fire and reload, and on the "Indian rush," in which soldiers dash from sheltered spot to sheltered spot, would have made assaults more successful. But soldiers hated to receive fire without shooting back, and the Indian rush was hard to control with a large army. Instead, although soldiers came to declare that "we dont mind the sight of dead men no more than if they was dead Hogs," they also grew more insistent on digging in for their own safety.

Volunteers had come to this war believing that courageous soldiers took the enemy's fire and kept moving forward until the foe retreated; if wounded, soldiers were to leave the field with a minimal display of pain. When the carnage of frontal assaults proved the folly of this belief, soldiers forced a change in tactics. Although early in the war some officers and enlisted men alike had sneered at trenches as a passive substitute for real fighting, most enlisted men came to prefer digging in to making frontal assaults. Indeed, Grant's army dragged its feet at any repetition of the Cold Harbor assault, and the rest of the campaign for Petersburg and Richmond was fought largely from trenches. Trench warfare had its own dangers, especially from sharpshooters who picked off unsuspecting soldiers at long range, but troops found these risks preferable to the wholesale slaughter of an assault.

Although soldiers fought as members of fiercely loyal groups and depended on comrades for their lives ("small-unit cohesion" in the language of military scholars), they also found battle to be an intensely personal experience. Soldiers were astonished at the mass confusion of the battlefield— some soldiers got lost, others panicked, troops with no idea of where to go got in the way of those who did know where they were going, and friend and foe blended into one another in a wildly changing melee. At the same time the senses were heightened during a battle. A private from Massachusetts wrote that "the air was filled with a medley of sounds, shouts, cheers, commands, oaths, the sharp report of rifles, the hissing shot, dull heavy thuds of clubbed muskets, the swish of swords and sabers, groans and prayers." And battles often turned into desperate personal combat with the enemy. These close-quarters fights provided most of the acts that were awarded medals, such as Samuel Eddy's shooting of a Confederate who had pinned him to the ground with a bayonet, and the horseback charge of an artillery sergeant at Gettysburg, slashing with his sword at onrushing Confederates.

Troops were acutely aware of those who "showed the white feather" and ran away during a battle. Straggling was most common early in the war, when untested volunteers found themselves unable to face enemy fire. If they had previously hidden their doubts with boastfulness, shirkers received the special scorn of their fellows. A Wisconsin soldier declared that "the story about Lawtons being so brave was all a hoax. As soon as the battle [of Shiloh] commenced he was making for the river about as fast as his legs would carry him." Straggling could also become contagious. In the same battle a general reported having seen "cowering under the river bank when I crossed from 7,000 to 10,000 men frantic with fright and utterly demoralized."

But the troops whose performance was scrutinized above all others were the African Americans who took to the field beginning in late 1862. There was still considerable Northern hostility to a war against slavery, and whites at the front and at home doubted blacks' ability to make good soldiers. Some whites believed that blacks lacked the strength of character to fight in the face of enemy fire; others were convinced that blacks would fight too well—their unrestrained passions would lead them on a rampage against their former masters.

In reality, black troops fought with distinction beginning with several skirmishes in early 1863, but it would take major battles to win over skeptics. In May 1863 two black regiments were ordered to attack a well-fortified Confederate force at Port Hudson, Louisiana, on the Mississippi River. Without artillery support or reinforcements, the black troops advanced against Confederate fire several times until it became clear that the enemy could not be dislodged. This was yet another failed assault for the Union, but the African-American troops had fought gallantly despite suffering 20 percent casualties.

Less than two months later, black troops faced a Confederate assault at Milliken's Bend, upriver from Port Hudson. Confederates reached the Union lines and fought the black troops hand to hand. When the enemy gained an edge, two companies of whites ran away, but the black troops held their ground; with the help of gunboats they forced the Confederates to break off the attack, but the black troops had suffered 35 percent casualties.

Then on July 18, the Fifty-fourth Massachusetts (Colored) Infantry led an assault on Fort Wagner outside Charleston, South Carolina. This was the elite among black regiments, led by Robert Gould Shaw, son of a leading antislavery family, and included two sons of Frederick Douglass. As the Fifty-fourth advanced on the fort, it was squeezed onto a narrow strip of land between a swamp and the ocean, making the troops an easy target for Confederate muskets and cannon in the fort. Shaw was killed, 40 percent of his soldiers died or were wounded, and the survivors were forced to retreat.

But doubts about blacks' ability and willingness to fight were all but extinguished. Full equality was not around the corner: African-American troops continued to receive shoddy weapons and inferior medical care, and there were reports of Union troops assaulting and shooting at black soldiers. Yet the *New York Times* acknowledged the beginning of a "prodigious revolution [in] the public mind." Advocates of equal rights pointed to the difference between black soldiers' valor on the battlefield and their treatment elsewhere; as a result, by the end of the war some states had empowered blacks to testify in court and to qualify for poor relief, and a few cities had ended segregation of their streetcars.

For black soldiers and whites alike, the days after a battle were a special form of misery. The end of a battle meant the start of the grisly task of tending to the wounded and burying the dead, who were often the friends and relatives of those doing the burying. Comrades or stretcher-bearers helped some of the wounded to the nearest cart or ambulance wagon, and the rest made their own way to the tent, barn, or farmhouse that served as a field hospital. For further treatment or recuperation, soldiers would eventually be moved by rail to a general hospital far behind the lines. Civil War hospitals were more dangerous than the battlefield: more deaths from wounds and disease occurred there than in battle. As disease performed its grim weeding-out of more susceptible men, sickness actually decreased—the rate of illness among soldiers dropped by 40 percent during the war. Nonetheless, twice as many Union soldiers died of disease as were killed by Confederate fire.

The creation of a hospital system to treat sick and wounded soldiers was a remarkable achievement. Starting with almost nothing, federal officials put together an organization that treated more than a million soldiers, operated more than two hundred general hospitals, and employed thirteen thousand physicians. The effort was aided by the United States Sanitary Commission, a quasi-official group of physicians and women reformers who investigated medical conditions in the army and advised officials on improvements. The commission also raised money to buy medical supplies for the troops and recruited women to serve as nurses in army hospitals.

Hospitals were nonetheless frightening places for sick or wounded soldiers. Knowing little about the causes of disease, the most physicians could do was to administer substances that seemed to stimulate the body to rid itself of the disturbance. Typhoid, for example, was often treated with calomel, a compound of mercury that stimulated the bowels, and malaria with ipecac, a plant extract that induced vomiting. In spite of these treatments, some soldiers managed to recover.

But it was the handling of wounds that was most associated with Civil War hospitals. The minié ball that was the mainstay of Civil War troops made a particularly menacing wound. Large, soft, and relatively slow-moving, the bullet usually lodged in the body, bringing along bits of clothing and hair and nearly always causing an infection. Due to soldiers' inaccuracy and to their eagerness to stay behind fortifications, two-thirds of wounds were in the limbs rather than the torso; this was fortunate because it avoided high-risk chest and abdominal surgery, but it also created the dilemma of what to do with shattered and infected limbs.

Physicians were caught between advocates of "conservative" treatment who urged saving a wounded arm or leg whenever possible (and risking the spread of life-threatening infection) and advocates of amputation to stop infection. Accounts of amputated arms and legs piled outside hospitals caused a public outcry and produced a shift toward the conservative approach by surgeons, but rough handling of wounds in the field and enormous numbers of wounded continued to encourage amputations. Union surgeons cut off thirty thousand arms and legs during the war, under conditions such as these reported by a witness:

> As a wounded man was lifted on the table, often shrieking with pain as the attendants handled him, the surgeon quickly examined the wound and resolved upon cutting off the injured limb. Some ether was administered and the body put in position in a moment. The surgeon snatched his knife from between his teeth . . . , wiped it rapidly once or twice across his bloodstained apron, and the cutting began. The operation accomplished, the surgeon would look around with a deep sigh, and then—"Next!"

But hospitals were not only places of torture. Physicians did what they could to relieve pain, liberally dispensing opium and morphine (and creating addicts in the process). They also made occasional, if haphazard, headway against infection. Although the actual nature and spread of infection would not be known until after the war, physicians did notice and sometimes made use of the disinfectant powers of substances such as iodine and carbolic acid.

And human compassion could be found in hospitals. Indeed, it was here that soldiers found the clearest reminders of home. Several thousand women worked as paid or volunteer nurses in Union army hospitals, and "we fell into maternal relations with [the men], ... addressing them individually as 'my son,' 'my boy,' or 'my child.'" If anything, the patients were even more eager for the mother-son relationship, and soldiers slipped easily into addressing their nurses as "Mother." Soldiers longed for the nurturance and moral authority they associated with womanhood, and so a nurse, according to an observer, "was almost an object of worship by those wholly excluded from home influences."

The absence of women's influence added insult to another kind of confinement for soldiers. Nearly 200,000 Union troops were held at one time or another as prisoners of war in the South, most of them in the war's later years. At first prisoners were exchanged under commanders' informal arrangements; if there were too many prisoners to hold until an exchange was negotiated, they were typically released on promising they would not resume fighting until notified they had been officially "exchanged." The two sides formalized this practice in July 1862. But the agreement broke down in 1863, chiefly over the issue of black troops in the Union army. The Confederate government authorized enslaving captured black soldiers and executing their white officers for inciting a slave revolt. The

North held up exchanges to discourage Confederates from carrying out their policy; when the South refused to include black prisoners in any exchanges, trading of prisoners virtually ceased, and each side was forced to house an exploding population of captives.

Soldiers' most bitter condemnations of the war concern prisons, largely because, according to one ex-prisoner, "we felt our manhood crushed to the very earth." Men had expected to serve by codes of honor and courage and to show self-control in the army, but prison life denied them the chance. Conditions in Southern prisons were appalling; a Confederate government that did not have the resources to feed and supply its own troops was in no position to care for an enormous prison population. The best-known Confederate prison was by far the largest, near Andersonville, Georgia. Built in early 1864 as an unsheltered stockade for 10,000 men, Andersonville held 33,000 prisoners by the summer. Rations bore little resemblance to food, and sanitation and medical care were primitive; upward of 100 prisoners died each day at the peak of the prison's crowding.

For decades after the war, survivors would denounce everyone connected with the prison, but they were especially distressed by what it did to human behavior. Most soldiers had come to the army intending to demonstrate manhood, but nonhuman references abound instead in prison descriptions. "The animal predominates," wrote an Andersonville prisoner, who described his fellow prisoners as "so many snarly dogs" and "hungry wolves penned together." Another inmate admitted becoming "more like a Devil than a man." Honor and courage gave way to the law of the jungle as gangs of thieves took over the prison. The prisoners themselves eventually rounded up the ringleaders, hanged six, and beat to death three others. Little wonder that twenty years after the war an ex-prisoner called his confinement "a long, dark night of lingering horror."

The handling of prisoners was not the only aspect of army experience that changed during the course of the war. The makeup of the Union army changed, as did the attitudes of the soldiers themselves. By 1863 the army was the product of a whittling-down process. The men who were most vulnerable to disease had died or been discharged, and some who could not stand the horrors of combat were also gone. Civil War battles produced symptoms, such as difficulty in breathing or severe depression, that we now associate with combat fatigue. Army physicians often concluded that men with such symptoms were insane, prompting one doctor to declare that "the number of cases of insanity in our army is astonishing." Rigid rules on discharges, however, limited the number of men released for combat stress. Some soldiers took desperate measures to escape combat. Self-mutilation, such as shooting off a finger or shooting oneself in the foot, was a common occurrence when the war was going poorly for the Union.

But by far the most common way out of the war was desertion. Approximately 200,000 Union soldiers deserted during the war. Men were especially likely to desert if they had had no compelling reason to enlist until bounties and substitute pay became lucrative, or if they did not belong to what historian Judith Hallock calls cohesive communities. In her study of two New York townships, Hallock found that desertions were considerably more common among soldiers from the township that had a high rate of population turnover and provided little public assistance to soldiers' families, compared to a more generous and tightly knit neighboring township. Cohesive communities were more likely to shame deserters back into the army, and community aid gave soldiers less reason to fear for their family's sustenance.

Deserters were also men who were willing to risk punishment. An estimated two-fifths of Union deserters were caught and returned to their units. Early in the war, deserters, like those guilty of lesser offenses, typically were punished by their commanders. A deserter might be branded with a "D" on the hip or the cheek, have his head shaved, or be drummed out of the service. The rate of desertion kept climbing, however, and punishments became harsher as the war continued. Deserters were now routinely court-martialed; soldiers who had deserted to attend to their families were often imprisoned at hard labor, but repeat offenders or men who had gone over to the enemy could receive a death sentence.

The Union executed 267 soldiers during the war, and more than half were for desertion; numerous others were subjected to a mock execution with a last-minute reprieve. Military punishment of whatever sort was always conducted in full view of the offender's comrades. In an execution this included the prisoner's entire regiment, brigade, or division (a brigade was three to five regiments, a division two to five brigades). The prisoner (or prisoners, because multiple executions occurred), an armed party of guards, a firing squad, and a chaplain were brought before the assembled troops while a band played the "Dead March." The prisoner was then seated on a coffin or placed standing beside an open grave and had his final words with the chaplain. The charges were read, the firing squad put into position, and the order to fire given. The volley did not always kill the prisoner, however, and authorities learned through experience to have a second and sometimes a third squad ready for another volley. Indeed, a convicted deserter from Pennsylvania was still standing after the first volley, remained sitting against his coffin after the second, and fell dead only after the third squad had fired. Following an execution, the assembled troops were marched

past the body for a full appreciation of the wages of disobedience.

Yet the lesson began to lose its impact because soldiers became acclimated to death in all its forms. The idealistic civilians of 1861 and 1862 were in the later years battle-hardened
soldiers, toughened against emotion, drawn together by shared
danger and suffering, and alienated from those who did not
share their experience. "Men can get accustomed to anything,"
wrote a corporal from Rhode Island, "and the daily sight of
blood and mangled bodies so blunted their finer sensibilities as
almost to blot out all love, all sympathy from the heart."

One's comrades, however, were an exception to the feeling
of alienation. Foremost among these were a soldier's messmates—men belonging to small groups that chose their own
members and cooked and ate together. No loyalties in the
army were fiercer than those among messmates: they were
known to call their group a family and their messmates brothers, and a poem by a Union army private maintained that
"there's never a bond, old friend, like this—We have drank
from the same canteen."

There was also a solidarity among enlisted men that went
beyond the mess and the regiment and could even cross
enemy lines. Officers did all they could to prohibit fraternization between Union and Confederate troops, but informal
truces persisted, and probably increased, throughout the war.
A mutual respect for fighting ability grew year by year, as did
mutual empathy for the plight of the common soldier. When
their lines were close enough, soldiers frequently called a truce
and talked, traded, swam, drank, and gambled together.

But as acts of fraternity increased, so did acts of hatred.
Ideals of honor and courage had largely given way to doing
one's duty and staying alive, and though Union troops had
great admiration for veteran foot soldiers on both sides, they

took no pity on anyone who seemed not to share their values. This included new recruits and support troops, whom front-line soldiers assumed were "bounty-jumpers" (men who enlisted to collect a bounty, deserted, then enlisted again elsewhere). A New York combat veteran, witnessing a bombardment of men he assumed were bounty-jumpers, had this reaction: "I saw men fall, saw others mangled by chunks of shell, and saw one, stuck fairly by an exploding shell, vanish. Enormously pleased, I hugged my lean legs, and laughed."

The enemy also included unsupportive people back home. Soldiers detested the "carpet knights at home": antiwar Northern Democrats, whom one soldier labeled "cowardly skunks," and businessmen and politicians "scrambling for wealth or for office." A Wisconsin soldier expressed the wish that Robert E. Lee, whose Army of Northern Virginia invaded Pennsylvania in 1863, "could have had a month more among the people of Pennsylvania" to acquaint them with the hardships of war.

But soldiers could only fantasize about punishing Northern ingrates. When Southern soldiers and civilians aroused antagonism Union troops could fully unleash their fury. Northern soldiers went south with a low opinion of Southerners—most believed that Southern society consisted of a few aristocrats ruling over slaves and a degraded population of white farmers—but few Northerners anticipated fighting civilians as well as soldiers.

Soldiers presumed that the main function of civilians was to stay out of the way of the armies; to people in the South, however, Union troops were invaders, so Southerners engaged in a host of partisan activities. Some men became guerrillas, dropping their usual occupation and joining armed bands to harass Union troops, then melting back into the countryside. Confederate officials were ambivalent about such bands—the

government officially recognized guerrillas in the Partisan
Ranger Act of 1862, then reversed itself in 1864 at the urging
of Robert E. Lee and others—but guerrilla leaders attracted
sizable followings in states such as Missouri, Virginia, and
Tennessee, where there were large numbers of Union as well
as Confederate sympathizers. Guerrillas such as William
Clarke Quantrill, "Bloody Bill" Anderson, and John Singleton
Mosby became heroes to Confederates and a scourge to federals. Avoiding open combat between equal forces, guerrillas
ambushed Union troops and murdered Unionist civilians.
There were reports of victims with their genitals cut off, and
members of Anderson's band carried scalps in their bridles.

Union soldiers were especially angered by the ease with
which guerrillas vanished into the civilian population. Guerrillas often operated out of their homes, and when confronted,
according to an Illinois soldier, "they are good union men &
unless you catch them in the very act you dont know who they
are." When guerrillas were away from home, Confederate
supporters fed and sheltered them, then pleaded innocence to
Union soldiers; families often switched loyalties depending on
who held sway in their neighborhood.

Nor, Union soldiers thought, could they trust Southern
women. Soldiers expected women to be nurturing and sub-
missive, and Southern women often were, nursing and feeding Union troops when they were in need. But other women
were openly defiant and occasionally dangerous. Women
jeered at Union prisoners, spat at the flag, and cursed occupy-
ing troops; they took shots at, and occasionally killed, Union
soldiers, led Yankees into guerrilla ambushes, and rode as
guerrillas themselves. Union troops thus operated in a murky
world in which social roles were turned upside down, everyone seemed to be the enemy, and sudden death could come
from anywhere.

And so Yankee soldiers acted less and less from civility and more from hatred for civilians. "Foraging" evolved from taking crops, livestock, and firewood that ill-supplied troops needed, into full-scale pillaging. William T. Sherman formalized the practice for his march through Georgia and the Carolinas that began in 1864, but Union soldiers across the South had already started turning foraging into punishment. Depending on their mood and on the reputed Confederate sympathies of their target, Union foragers took corn and grain, confiscated livestock, and broke into houses for clothing, furniture, and jewelry. Officers expressed only token disapproval. Victims who were particularly defiant might have their houses burned. Union troops found that burning an enemy's house both demonstrated the army's power to exact vengeance and underscored the owner's powerlessness.

Yet there were restraints on these Union soldiers' attacks on civilians. In the twentieth century we are accustomed to hearing reports of assaults on enemy women, especially rape. Union troops did commit rape in the Civil War, and eighteen soldiers were executed for the crime. Executions are only the vaguest clue to a crime's prevalence, but historians have concluded that surprisingly little rape took place during the Civil War, and that there was even less against white women. Union soldiers could simultaneously humiliate Southerners and show their hatred for African Americans by raping black women who were under whites' control, and there are reports that some soldiers did so. Yet Union soldiers, disillusioned as they were, retained some self-control and some reverence for womanhood.

Few restraints were evident, however, in soldiers' treatment of guerrillas. Union soldiers adopted the guerrillas' own tactics, using informers, wearing civilian clothes to infiltrate guerrilla bands, and torturing and executing prisoners as they caught them. To bolster their confidence against guerrillas' intimidation, Union troops adopted language from their hunting days. A colonel in Missouri referred to his assignment "of hunting and in some cases exterminating bushwhackers," and another officer boasted that "my men say they can track the bushmen like a dog would a deer." Fighting guerrillas became an eye-for-an-eye struggle of stealth and vengeance.

Atrocities by Confederate regulars similarly triggered the wrath of Union troops. Soldiers' respect for persistence in doing one's duty did not extend to wanton killing. After the introduction of black troops, some Confederates went beyond their government's threats and shot down captured black soldiers on the spot. Documented instances of such murders were isolated until a massacre of black soldiers occurred at Fort Pillow, Tennessee, in April 1864. General Nathan Bedford Forrest and his Confederate cavalry captured the fort and then killed as many as a hundred black troops among the garrison. News of the killings infuriated African Americans throughout the army, and Union troops, black and white, occasionally gunned down Confederate captives with a cry of "Remember Fort Pillow!"

Yet despite their bitter disillusionment most Union soldiers still clung to a few ideals they could separate from the battlefield. On the same evening that messmates vehemently denounced cowards and profiteers back home, they might also wipe away tears as they sang "Home, Sweet Home"; soldiers usually exempted their own families from condemnations of the home front. Or a soldier might take a gold watch from a dying enemy and then write home about his duty to save the Union; there was no appreciable decline in soldiers' expressions of patriotism even as they abandoned rules of civility.

Patriotism and duty were, however, pushed to the limit in 1864, when men with three-year enlistments from 1861 were scheduled to go home. Taking no chances, the federal government offered a month-long furlough, a bonus, and other incentives to induce soldiers to reenlist. Approximately 100,000 men declined the offer and served out their enlistment, but nearly 140,000 others signed on for three more years. A higher percentage of men thus reenlisted than had enlisted in the first place, and historians generally emphasize the importance of duty to comrades and country in convincing soldiers to reenlist.

Yet patriotism probably had little to do with the high rate of reenlistment decisions. For many soldiers the lure of furlough was irresistible. As one Ohio officer put it, it was worth trading "three years more of hell" for "thirty days of heaven—home." Bounties were also enormously attractive to men whose families were going hungry in their absence, but the government used threats as well as enticements to persuade the undecided. Soldiers who were vocal in discouraging reenlistment faced arrest, and men who refused to reenlist were to be classified as "non-veterans" when they were discharged. Most of those who reenlisted undoubtedly did so for this combination of desires and pressures that the government had cleverly exploited.

In 1865 a soldier in Sherman's army wrote that "the experience of twenty years of peaceful life has been crowded into three years." He and his Northern comrades had seen young men die in numbers they could not have imagined earlier, and few of them were good deaths. They had also suffered from fear, hunger, and disease in ways that were inconceivable before the war, and that, in their view, no one else could ever understand. Yet soldiers had also influenced the way the war was fought. Their growing resistance to frontal assaults forced commanders to modify their tactics, and soldiers' evolving detachment about inflicting suffering helped to make possible Sherman's march through Georgia and the Carolinas. And black soldiers, besides being instrumental in the siege of Petersburg, the defense of Nashville, and other late-war battles, erased some of their white comrades' racism and inspired new resolve among jaded white troops. On several occasions whites raised a cheer for black soldiers' performance, and one white officer paid blacks a soldier's tribute: blacks' gallantry, he declared, "will have established their manhood."

Enlisted men were in a poor position to gauge the course of the war. Union troops saw by 1865 that Confederate soldiers were ragged and demoralized, but Yankees were often little better off. Soldiers were passionately interested in knowing when the end would come, but most of their information came from rumors they had long since learned to distrust. Their concerns were also personal—how they had performed in the most recent fight, whether they would survive the next one, whether they would find something better than hardtack (an essentially inedible biscuit) for their next meal, and how to get some decent shoes. Sherman's soldiers, for example, were preparing in North Carolina for yet another campaign when the latest round of rumors proved to be true: the Confederates were surrendering, and the war was over.

These were the experiences of the victors. Fighting for a nation of immense resources whose economy boomed during the war, Union soldiers nonetheless acquired physical and psychological scars from the fighting. How did their experience compare with that of Confederates?

4

Confederates at War

FEW CONFEDERATE RECRUITS expected to meet an honorable foe. The North, they believed, would copy the practice of the British in the American Revolution: Yankees would search the streets and the saloons to produce an army "filled up with the scum of creation" and would probably add a "hireling host" of European mercenaries to plunder the South. The Southern army, by contrast, made up of "the best blood of the grand old Southland," would have little trouble defeating this rabble.

To get the chance, however, the recruits would need to become soldiers, which meant putting up with camp life. Like Union troops, Confederate soldiers went to camps of instruction for initial training and later made camp for wintertime lulls in the fighting. While they were there, officers tried to instill discipline through drill and rules for behavior, but they fell into a contest of wills with their soldiers that was probably sharper than in the Union army. For one thing, among the Confederate officers there were more professional soldiers. At the beginning of the war, experienced Union officers were kept in the regular army while their Southern peers were resigning to train Confederate volunteers; other Confederate officers came from military schools, almost all of which were in the South. These trained officers were especially likely to demand military discipline among their troops.

But Southern enlisted men were especially poor candidates for this discipline. They came from a society that prepared white men to give orders, not take them. The result was, a Virginia soldier concluded, "an individual who could not become the indefinite portion of a mass, but fought for himself, on his own account." Such an individual reserved for himself "the right of private judgment" on orders he received, and he had a familiar standard of unacceptable treatment—being ordered about like a slave. A Georgia volunteer thus complained that "a private soldier is nothing more than a slave and is often treated worse," and another soldier declared that he was "tired of being bound up worse than a negro."

Confederates elected their officers: companies voted for lieutenants and captains, who in turn chose regimental officers. The government tried to phase out the practice, but it lingered in some units until the war's end. When one of these public servants ordered a soldier to dig a latrine it was bad enough, but when he had the soldier thrown in the guard-house for disputing the order it was an affront to a man's honor. A Tennessee private thus refused to take part in a drill and then threatened the officer who tried to reprimand him; a Louisiana soldier responded to an order by insisting he was a gentleman and drawing a sword on his lieutenant; and another soldier, threatened with punishment for disobedience, called the officer involved "a damned coward," promising that "if you will pull off your insignia of rank I will whip you on the spot."

Confederate soldiers did not, however, hate all officers. Historians Joseph Frank and George Reaves found that only a few more Confederates than Yankees complained about their officers' military competence at Shiloh. Pete Maslowski's

sample of soldiers' testimony found that Confederate enlisted
men appreciated their officers' personal interest in them. But
that appreciation could quickly explode into rage when an
officer betrayed the mutual respect that Southern soldiers
expected.

Confederate enlisted men also resisted limits on their off-
duty behavior. Gambling was as popular in Confederate
camps as it was among Yankees: some Southern soldiers
would take a chance on anything, from the roll of dice to the
outcome of a louse race. Drinking was similarly widespread.
Commanders punished soldiers for drunkenness and banned
the sale of liquor in or near their camps, but the prohibition
only inspired more ingenuity in finding and smuggling liquor.
One company brought in liquor in a hollowed-out water-
melon, and a Tennessee soldier smuggled in a supply of
whiskey in the barrel of his gun. Another soldier recalled that
"in each regiment there were a few men who could find a still-
house if it was within twenty miles of the line of march."

Like Northern units, Southern companies consisted of
friends, relatives, and neighbors from the same community
(at least until attrition forced consolidation of units late in
the war), but Southern soldiers felt the same dissatisfaction
with their all-male world as did Yankees, and they tried the
same remedies. Some Confederates made do with polite
social visits or all-male dances, but others preferred to defy
their commanders and seek sexual satisfaction with prostitutes whenever they had the chance. It is impossible to determine whether Confederates went to prostitutes as often as
did Yankees, but it is likely that Southerners had fewer
opportunities: they were less often camped near cities, many
of which were in Union hands anyway, and runaway infla-
tion made Confederate money worth less than Union green-
backs. Yet commanders were certainly convinced that

prostitution was a major problem. Their response was to take action against the women: some officials investigated the character of camp followers, including cooks and laundresses, and one general ordered a sweep of a Georgia town, with orders to banish or imprison women of suspicious reputation. There is little evidence, however, that any of these measures worked.

Confederate officials never fully came to terms with the right of private judgment. To be sure, the army had its advocates of iron discipline: Stonewall Jackson refused to lighten court-martial punishments of his troops, and Robert E. Lee asserted that "hundreds of lives have been needlessly sacrificed for want of a strict observance of discipline." But day-to-day dealings with touchy enlisted men discouraged officers from harsh punishment. The soldier who called his officer a "damned coward," for example, was not punished for his outburst, and in the case of one Louisiana private caught sleeping on guard duty, a court-martial imposed a light sentence on the grounds that he had been drunk that night. What one historian has called the Confederates' "prevailing custom of leniency" undoubtedly came from the knowledge that Southern men could and did rebel against severe punishment, especially from unpopular officers. Virginia soldiers, for example, refused to submit to punishment by the "tyrannical" General Charles Winder, and General Allison Nelson's men fired into his tent, thereby convincing him to release two comrades from punishment.

But appealing as defiance of authority was, Confederate soldiers were also as eager as Yankees to duplicate features of family and community in camp. Confederates likewise formed messes, whose bonds were recalled by a Virginia veteran. A soldier, he wrote, "learns to look upon [his comrades] as brothers; there is no sacrifice he will not make for them; no trouble that he will not cheerfully take. Fellowship becomes almost a religion."

Soldiers had a variety of ways to replicate the larger community as well. Some armies published newspapers, which could be handwritten sheets such as "The Pioneer Banner," published by Alabamians, or printed papers such as the *Missouri Army Argus*. Other soldiers arranged formal entertainments, which might be a concert by a regimental band or a burlesque staged by soldier-actors. Military theatricals could become elaborate: programs were occasionally printed, costumes and makeup improvised, and civilians invited. And Confederates were as preoccupied as Yankees with music, both formal and informal. Bands frequently accompanied the theatricals, and Louisiana and Kentucky companies performed an opera in 1864. Southerners also sang at every opportunity, supplementing songs such as "Home, Sweet Home" and "When This Cruel War Is Over" with "Dixie" and "The Bonnie Blue Flag."

Confederates engaged in most of the same sports as did Yankees—ball games, boxing, foot races, snowball fights, and so on—but Southern soldiers were especially devoted to hunting. As we have seen, many Northerners had hunted as civilians and some adapted hunting language to warfare, but Southerners held a special reverence for this ritual that allowed both competition and male companionship; moreover, they had an extra incentive to hunt when rations worsened during the war. Soldiers took whatever opportunities they could find to hunt in spite of the restrictions of army life. Prohibited from using valuable ammunition to hunt, Confederates stalked rabbits and partridges with clubs and climbed trees in search of squirrels. Soldiers would even break ranks in a drill or on the march when someone spotted game. A Virginia soldier recalled that when a rabbit burst into view, "regardless of officers' commands, the soldiers with one shout would start after him.... A strange characteristic of the Southern army was their insane desire to run a hare."

Religion was a feature of Southern communities about which soldiers were initially ambivalent. Evangelical religion—built around humans' personal relationship with God and preoccupied with overcoming sin and achieving an assured salvation—was a pillar of Southern communal life, but it could run afoul of masculine culture. Young men expected preachers to rail against sin, but they also expected the chance to act like men, especially in the army. If this meant a friendly game of cards and a drink or two, and maybe answering an insult with one's fists, that was what men did; few young men expected to die soon, so there was plenty of time to make amends. As a result, the most vivid descriptions of Confederate sinfulness came from chaplains who were appalled by what they saw and heard. A Mississippi chaplain complained that among his comrades were "the most vile, obscene blackguards that could be raked up this side [of] the bad place.... From early morn to dewey eve there is one uninterrupted flow of the dirtiest talk I ever heard in my life." Chaplains would have agreed with another Mississippian that "it is an uphill and discouraging business preaching to Soldiers," and many resigned; by 1862 it was estimated that only half of Confederate units had a chaplain.

But however much Confederates tried to replicate the society they had left, they were also anxious to get into the field and get on with the fighting. Infantry drill, which filled Southerners' days as it did Yankees', made Confederates equally impatient to get out of camp. Frustrated officers drilling reluctant soldiers produced scenes of exasperation similar to those in the North. In a Virginia company, "the luckless captain, losing what little self-possession he had, blundered more and more and generally ended up tying his company in a hard knot."

And Southern soldiers were nearly as unprepared to shoot effectively. Like Union troops, many Southern recruits brought their own weapons, but Confederate authorities had a much harder time replacing them and equipping men who were unarmed. Few weapons were manufactured in the Confederacy, so the government had to buy most of its guns in Europe and try to run them through the Union blockade of Confederate ports. Some states had adequate supplies of guns and a few had surpluses, but governors refused to allow Richmond to distribute their extras. As a result, Confederate soldiers early in the war were armed with a bewildering array of weapons—flintlock muskets that would not fire in the rain, hunting rifles, smoothbore muskets, shotguns, and pistols—and many men were still unarmed. The lack of guns was worst in the war's first year: western commanders reported in the winter of 1861–1862 that up to half their troops had no weapons.

Supplies improved by the next year as Southerners captured large numbers of Springfield rifled muskets and began receiving shipments of the similar English-made Enfields. By 1864 more than 80 percent of soldiers in the Army of Tennessee, for example, had the potentially accurate rifled musket. But even though many Southerners had been good shots with their own weapons, they had little chance to develop much skill with the new guns. Confederate officers were as reluctant as Northerners to use up ammunition and risk accidents in target practice, and Southern soldiers were likewise hampered by battlefield smoke. Rebels' small-arms fire was probably more accurate than was Northerners', but Paddy Griffith has nonetheless estimated that Confederates fired a hundred shots for every one that hit a Yankee.

A number of Southern recruits never got the chance to test their prowess against the enemy. Disease attacked first, racing through Confederate camps and killing a larger proportion of soldiers than in the North. More Confederates came from rural areas with no exposure and thus no immunity to common diseases, so Southern units would typically lose more men before engaging the enemy. Southerners who survived this first assault by disease went through most of the same preparations for battle as did Yankees: sometimes a train trip toward the next campaign, more often a march during which soldiers finished "simmering down" to the minimum of equipment. When they had reached the place where the generals expected a battle, the troops received their ammunition and rations and were stationed to attack or to hold a position. The commanding officer would give his speech, and the troops would wait for the battle to begin.

In major battles Confederates were more likely than Union troops to be ordered into a frontal assault. As with Union assaults, Southern troops would be arranged in two or more lines that were supposed to keep a good distance apart. Occasionally Civil War armies attacked in columns rather than these broad rows, but commanders preferred to send their troops elbow-to-elbow against the enemy, with orders to finish with a bayonet charge.

Historians are divided about why Confederate leaders were especially anxious to use assaults. They do agree on the South's commitment to offensive warfare. A Richmond newspaper insisted that "waiting for blows, instead of inflicting them, is altogether unsuited to the genius of our people"; Confederate President Jefferson Davis endorsed "the one great object of giving to our columns capacity to take the offensive"; and a Confederate officer longed for warfare that "hurls masses against . . . the enemy's army." And Southerners acted on their commitment: they were the attackers in eight of the war's first twelve major battles. But the cause of these views is less clear. The South's aggressiveness has been variously attributed to West Point training, to the successful use of assaults in the Mexican War, and, in an intriguing study by Grady McWhiney and Perry Jamieson, to the influence of Europe's fierce Celtic people on the American South. Other historians have pointed out that in smaller engagements Union forces were just as likely to attack as were Confederates.

There is little disagreement, however, about the cost of their assaults to the Confederates. In the eight major battles with the South as aggressor, the Confederates had nearly one-fourth of their men killed, wounded, or captured, while the Union lost only 15 percent of its troops. Confederate generals deemphasized but never abandoned assaults later in the war. In 1864 John Bell Hood lost more than eleven thousand men in two frontal assaults near Atlanta, then lost five thousand more in an attack at Franklin, Tennessee, while the defending Yankees were losing one-third as many soldiers.

Since Confederates were especially committed to the assault, it is appropriate to view a typical charge from a Southern viewpoint, though the experiences were similar whichever side was on the offensive. Waiting for the order to charge was a special ordeal, especially for untested soldiers. Men who had "seen the elephant," the popular term for undergoing combat, might appear calm and even catch a nap if the waiting dragged on, but new soldiers were usually tormented with doubts about their performance. No one knew if he would be killed or wounded, of course, but untested soldiers did not even know if they would be paralyzed with fear; this is why officers promised to shoot anyone who broke ranks during an assault. If the Yankees were already firing their artillery, the fear was that much worse: one soldier under cannon fire re-called his hair "standing on end like the quills of a porcupine."

The command to advance was a kind of liberation. Soldiers could now take on those Yankees whose guns and bayonets they could see while they waited. The attackers marched in their lines, often across an open field, and they could not wait to take their first shot. Officers, realizing that stopping to fire a volley made soldiers better targets, frequently pleaded with their men not to shoot, but firing at the enemy was crucial for a soldier. "With your first shot you become a new man," wrote a Confederate. "Personal safety is your least concern. Fear has no existence in your bosom." The charge quickly became a combination of grim determination and sudden shock. A Tennessee officer recalled that "I do not remember that on our way across the open space, a command was given or a word spoken. 'Where is the enemy?' I kept asking myself." And then "the fence before us became transformed into a wall of flame." As the Yankees fired on the Orleans Guard of Louisiana, a volunteer measured his progress by his downed comrades: "Porce down . . . Gallot down . . . Coiron, arm shat-tered . . . Percy wounded." A Mississippi lieutenant acknowl-edged only one honorable way out of this horror: "The first wounded man I recognized was my Uncle Henry's eldest son, cousin James Mangum. He had been shot in the face. I wanted to help him [but] everyone was moving forward. . . . We just had to get at those Federals who were shooting us."

Any semblance of coordination usually disappeared in an assault. The carefully separated lines often collapsed into a disorganized crowd. Soldiers seldom used their bayonets; if enough Confederates reached the Union lines, the assault would probably end as did the Orleans Guard's ("A ragged stand up volley at the Unionists and they scramble off"). But more often, attacks ended like another assault witnessed by

the Guard. This time a regiment disappeared over a rise toward the Union position, and soon "the decomposed line
tumbled back over the crest again. Men scarcely could be recognized ... shirts covered with blood ... faces disfigured
with hideous wounds."

Unsuccessful attackers might be ordered to regroup and try
again the same day or on following days. When the fighting
ended, a mixture of exhaustion, shock, and depression over-
came the soldiers. Fatigue was overpowering after a battle,
and men often collapsed at night amid corpses that were too
numerous to bury. But soldiers also had to come to grips with
the carnage they had participated in. Writing about what they
saw after a battle, Confederates expressed the same horrified
wonderment as did Yankees. A Georgia soldier, for example,
described a field where "stiffened bodies lie, grasping in death
the arms they bravely bore, with glazed eyes, and features
blackened by rapid decay. . . . The air is putrid with decaying
bodies of men & horses." And win or lose, soldiers' emotions
easily slid into depression. Confederates were especially forth-
right in admitting their despondency. John Taylor of Tennessee, in retreat from Murfreesboro, watched as "tears traced
each other down [the] manly cheeks" of his comrades, and a
Louisiana soldier saw that there were "tears stealing down the
cheeks of nearly all present" at a prayer service for the dead.
The feelings themselves were shared on both sides: nearly
three-fourths of the soldiers studied by Frank and Reaves expressed despair after the Battle of Shiloh.

The trauma of battle for unharmed men, however, paled
beside the terror and misery of the wounded. Wounded men
might lie on the battlefield for hours, sometimes for days, before stretcher-bearers reached them; if the army was in retreat
when they were picked up, they would have to endure a long,
rough ride before getting medical attention. On the retreat

from Gettysburg, an officer in Lee's army saw that "torn and bloody clothing, matted and hardened, was rasping the tender, inflamed, and still oozing wounds" of men riding a wagon; he heard one man cry, "For God's sake, stop just for one minute; take me out and leave me to die on the roadside."

Wounded men were little better off when they did reach a hospital. Confederate physicians, like their Union counterparts, had already been fighting a losing battle against disease when they were overwhelmed by combat casualties. The crisis was worse in the Confederate army, which had one surgeon per 324 men compared with the Union's one per 133 (though local physicians helped the Confederates when they could). Confederate surgeons also had to make do with fewer supplies than did Union physicians.

But given medical science's ignorance of the causes underlying disease and infections, shortages of physicians and supplies could prove a blessing. Wounds crawling with maggots, for example, horrified both victims and physicians, and Union surgeons scrupulously removed maggots when they appeared. Yet maggots are efficient cleansers, eating infected tissue while leaving healthy flesh alone. Neglect by frantically overworked medical personnel may thus have saved Confederates such as John Dooley, who lay for days after Gettysburg with maggot-infested wounds. Indeed, despite the difference in physicians and supplies, the Confederate death rate from wounds appears to have been only marginally higher than the 15 percent estimated for Union troops.

Confederate surgeons often performed heroically under impossible conditions. Like Union physicians, some were drunks and some were uncaring, but others were praised as "constant [and] kind" and "a true friend and a Christian Soldier." Hundreds of Southern women served as nurses and hospital matrons, brushing aside initial resistance to their crossing the barrier between female and male worlds. They filled the same maternal role as Northern nurses did, and drew this praise from a Virginia soldier: "May God ever bless them, from the maiden of sixty to the young girl in her teens, [as they] moved like ministering angels among these sufferers." But no amount of care could heal the despondency of some hospitalized soldiers. An observer described the typical sight of a soldier who "had grown hopeless and despairing" in the hospital. "He had lost all control over himself and would cry like a child." Soon he would die "because he had not nervous force enough to hold on to the attenuated thread of life."

Imprisonment caused a different sort of despair among Southern soldiers. Where sickness and wounds made them helpless at the hands of Southerners, capture put Confederates at the mercy of their enemies, leaving them vulnerable to insults and dishonor. The Union housed its prisoners in a variety of forts and stockades, and its policies were guided less by available resources than by reports of conditions at Confederate prisons; indeed, the Union commissary-general of prisons returned $2 million to the federal treasury at war's end. As the Confederacy cut rations for the prisoners it held (and for its troops in the field), the North did likewise for its prisoners. Northern officials and civilians nonetheless believed they were pampering their captives, and they were galled by tales of "sleek fat rebels" in Union prisons. Southerners, for their part, were angered by what they saw as deliberate mistreatment of prisoners in a land of plenty.

Southern prisoners were highly sensitive to the attitude of their captors and were quick to commend officials they saw as honorable. The commandant of Johnson's Island in Lake Erie was praised as "a good friend to the prisoners," and former prisoners paid for a bust to honor the Camp Morton, Indiana, prison head. But far more often inmates denounced Northern prison officials as vicious and corrupt. Officials were accused of shooting prisoners without provocation, soliciting bribes and then punishing the takers, and encouraging African-American guards to humiliate inmates.

Prison stories on both sides were typically exaggerated, but the North did have its own version of Andersonville in the stockade at Elmira, New York, built in 1864 and described by a Texas inmate as "hell on earth." Prisoners, characterized by a camp official as "pale and emaciated, hollow-eyed and dispirited," were crowded into barracks and tents that gave little protection from the bitter winter of 1864–1865. Scurvy, dysentery, pneumonia, and smallpox were epidemic, and 25 percent of Elmira's prisoners died, a rate lower than Andersonville's toll of more than 30 percent but nonetheless much worse than the chances of death in battle. Trapped between the continual presence of death and the hope of a prisoner exchange that never came, many inmates of Northern prisons shared the dejection of this North Carolina soldier: "Oh, God, how dreadful are these bitter feelings of hope deferred. I sink almost in madness and despair."

Confederates who stayed out of prison and the hospital underwent changes as well. Southerners became as battle-hardened as Union troops. Samuel Foster, a Texas officer, reported that artillery fire "amounts to nothing. Shelling don't scare us as it used to"; another soldier admitted that gruesome sights "do not affect me as they once did. . . . I look on the carcass of a man now with pretty much the same feeling as I would do were it a horse or hog." And like Yankee soldiers, Confederates began to resist reckless tactics. Soldiers knew that frontal assaults as they were practiced made them easy targets, and their tolerance for such tactics declined.

As early as 1862 a Texas soldier declared that he was "satis-

fied not to make another such charge" as the one at Gaines's
Mill in Virginia. Soldiers' opposition to assaults became increasingly bitter: Samuel Foster charged that John Bell Hood
"virtually murdered 10,000 men around Atlanta" in 1864.
And the men did not simply complain. At Ezra Church,
Georgia, in the same year, the Confederate commander acknowledged that "the attack was a feeble one," and at nearby
Jonesboro a regiment refused to attack because "the men
seemed possessed of some great horror of charging breast-
works." These troops would later participate in the charge at
Franklin, but this would be an exception to soldiers' increasing reluctance to serve as cannon fodder. Like Union troops,
Confederates dug trenches more often as the war went on.
Enlisted men wanted to fight, in the words of a Virginia soldier, in "a very thin gray line ... back of a thin, red line of
clay." The high command continued to feel otherwise, which
inspired this cheer in the Army of Tennessee: "Hurrah [de-
fense-minded General] Joe Johnston and god D—m Jeff
Davis."

As defeats mounted and Union troops occupied more of
their territory, more Southerners turned to guerrilla warfare.
Guerrillas were not, of course, regular soldiers, but a substantial number of men became guerrillas at one time or another,
and their activities occupied troops and officials on both sides.
Indeed, there were guerilla attacks *against* as well as *for* the
Confederacy, but there were differences between the two
kinds of assault. Anti-Confederate attacks more easily shaded
into pure thievery. Renegade bands, frequently dominated by
Confederate deserters, roamed through areas as far apart as
the North Carolina mountains and the piney woods of southern Mississippi. Sometimes driven by hunger and sometimes
by criminal intent, these bands descended on houses and settlements, stealing anything of value and occasionally shooting

those who resisted, with little regard for victims' political sympathies.

Pro-Confederate guerrillas, who operated closer to Union armies, also did their share of pillaging and terrorizing, especially when they came across Unionists' dwellings. But they had partisan motives that caused them to see themselves as distinct from marauders. Most partisan guerrillas were young men who had not previously been in the Confederate army. William Clarke Quantrill was in his mid-twenties when he formed his guerrilla band; "Bloody Bill" Anderson, the leader of another Missouri band, was twenty when he was gunned down in 1864, and Joe Hart, a notorious guerrilla leader in northwestern Missouri, was eighteen at his death. As historian Michael Fellman points out, guerrillas rejected army discipline for a fancied role as knight-errant, protecting Southern citizens from Yankee savagery. They could tip their hats to women and dutifully write to their parents about their exploits because they were convinced they were simply answering the Yankees, atrocity for atrocity. Determined "to wage the most active war against our brutal invaders," guerrillas ambushed Union soldiers, murdered Unionist civilians, ransacked houses, and attacked churches, typically citing some provocation by the other side to justify themselves.

Guerrillas and renegades provoked increasingly brutal reprisals as the war went on. In 1863, for example, Union cavalrymen surrounded a number of guerrillas in Missouri, "and within fifteen minutes we had exterminated the whole band" except for three wounded men reluctantly taken prisoner. In another incident, Union troops in Tennessee put out the eyes of a captured guerrilla, cut out his tongue, dragged him from a horse until he was dead, and tied his body to a tree. For their part, Confederate troops in the North Carolina mountains, after using torture to extract information from local women, rounded up and shot thirteen suspected Unionist marauders, aged thirteen to sixty.

Battle-hardening among regular Confederate soldiers shaded into hatred for anyone who did not share their role, but with some differences from the Northern experience. Since there was widespread deprivation at home, Southern soldiers were slower to condemn the civilian populace in general than were Northerners; on the other hand, Confederates were quicker to denounce profiteers, those "cowardly scamps" who, according to a Tennessee soldier, preferred to "retire to their feathered couches . . . and ponder in their minds in what maner they can swindle the country."

Indeed, Confederate and Union soldiers had fundamentally different relationships with civilians. Yankees were in enemy territory: if they were exasperated by civilians' treachery, they could retaliate by looting and burning and then insist that the civilians had brought it on themselves. Yet these same civilians were the people Confederates were fighting for. Even if some civilians had more food than soldiers did, most were hardly wealthy; Confederate commanders discouraged plunder, and most of their men let civilians alone. Some soldiers, however, assumed that their country should support its defenders, and they tore down fences for firewood, commandeered livestock, and raided fields and gardens. Civilians were outraged: North Carolina's governor denounced the "half-armed, half-disciplined Confederate Cavalry" as a "plague worse than all others," and a Mississippi farmer lamented, "Lord deliver me from our friends."

Some Confederate soldiers did get the chance to confront Northern civilians. The best-known encounter was General Lee's invasion of Pennsylvania in the summer of 1863. To demonstrate that Confederates were honorable soldiers and not plunderers, Lee tried to keep his men on a tight rein. The soldiers themselves reacted to this glimpse of enemy territory in much the same way as did Yankees in the South. Some Southerners expressed surprise at Pennsylvania's prosperity and admired its people, echoing some Yankee comments on the South. Other Confederates, however, recited criticisms that were essentially a script for Civil War soldiers. As Reid Mitchell points out, if you wanted to disparage your enemies, you sneered at their cleanliness and the appearance of their women. Yankees did it in the South, and now it was the Confederates' turn. A North Carolina general declared that Pennsylvania residents were "coarse and dirty and the number of dirty-looking children is perfectly astonishing," and another soldier claimed that the state had "the largest collection of ugly dirty looking women I ever saw."

When they could avoid the watchful eye of their commanders, many of Lee's soldiers acted in much the same way as they believed Yankees did on Southern soil. Some Confederates could not resist the temptation to take whatever they could carry. A Virginia officer wrote a letter from Pennsylvania, "sitting by a fine rail fire"; he reported that "in spite of orders, [the men] step out at night and help themselves to milk, butter, poultry, and vegetables." Some Confederates went further: to underscore their prowess, they rounded up ex-slaves and free blacks for sale into slavery. These soldiers were willing to defy their leaders to assert Southern power and avenge what they considered to be Yankee cruelties in the South.

As they retreated from their foray into Pennsylvania, more and more of Lee's soldiers thought about religion. Despite the disillusionment, even resignation, of many Confederate chaplains during the early phase of the war, the continued bloodletting sparked a religious revival that swept the Confederate army. In the fall of 1862, after a northward thrust had been turned back at Antietam, Maryland, religious services in Lee's

army began to draw ever larger and more enthusiastic
turnouts, and the chaplains who were still on hand found they
could hardly keep up with requests for prayer services. Local
clergymen helped with the preaching, and soldiers showed increasing interest in the religious literature that was distributed
in camp. This revival was interrupted by the campaigning of
1863, but it resumed with increased enthusiasm and spread to
the western armies in the winter of 1863–1864. Soldiers across
the South built scores of chapels in their camps, crowded into
them or stood outdoors for services, and converted in large
numbers. Preachers would report a hundred conversions in a
good day, and one estimate puts the total number of Confederate converts at 150,000. "I have never seen such a spirit as
there is now in the army," wrote a Texas chaplain in 1864, and
a Louisiana surgeon reported that "from daylight until the
late hours of the night nothing is heard but hymns and pray-
ing."

Although revivals did occur in the Union army, they were
overshadowed by the Confederate awakening in both extent
and fervor. Union army conversions have been estimated at
about the same number as Confederate converts, but the
Union army was more than twice as large. Nor did revivals
occur on either home front to match those in the Confederate
army.

Why was this awakening primarily a Confederate army
event? The revivals have often been attributed to defeat and
death: defeats such as Antietam in 1862 and Gettysburg and
Vicksburg in 1863 seemed to many Confederates to be God's
punishments for their sins, and the carnage on the battlefield
made soldiers aware of death's closeness. Yet Lee's army won a
major victory at Fredericksburg, Virginia, in late 1862. This
victory failed to slow the Confederate revivals, and its appalling Union casualties, which caused commentators to label

the battle a "massacre" and a "disaster" for the Union, did not touch off comparable revivals on the other side. Not until the following spring did the more modest Union army awakening begin in earnest.

Historians assume that the accumulation of defeats contributed to the resumption of revivals in 1863–1864, though a Confederate victory at Chickamauga, Georgia, in September 1863 did little to impede the religious urgency. Historian Drew Faust has offered another explanation that helps to account for Confederates' exceptional spiritual interest. The personal, salvation-based religion that was so familiar to Southerners was an ideal remedy for combat stress. The façade of indifference that constituted battle-hardening reduced the outward show of fear, but many soldiers remained inwardly horrified at combat's waste of human lives and terrified of their own death. Instead of denying these emotions, evangelical religion allowed believers to acknowledge and transcend them. A personal assurance of salvation offered reason enough for enduring the mind-numbing terror of warfare: Southern soldiers would thus stand in the rain or in ankle-deep snow for a chance to hear sermons or wait patiently for a preacher to break through a frozen pond for baptisms. The whole thing was simple, according to a Tennessee soldier, who wrote to his wife that "the Cauze of [God's] being my friend [is that] I have ask him for his blessing." Death had lost its terror for him because "we will meat in heaven where there is no ware."

Northern religious beliefs, on the other hand, more often emphasized the individual's duty to state and nation; Union soldiers seldom referred to God as their friend. Reminders of duty did comfort soldiers like Pennsylvanian Milton Ray: "If it is [God's] will that I should sacrifice my life for my country then the Lord Jesus will receive my spirit. Pray that I may be a faithful soldier of the cross and of my country." Yet this belief attracted proportionally fewer soldiers than did the assurance that God was reaching out to provide a personal assurance of salvation to each Confederate believer.

But the consoling power of religion had its limits, even among Southern soldiers. The continuing toll of defeats, combined with worsening shortages of supplies, eventually pushed soldiers beyond the reach of preachers' assurances. Religious enthusiasm among Confederates subsided, especially in the West. Few mentions of chaplains have been found in late-war writings of soldiers. Virginian Alexander Hunter explained: "It is hard to retain religion on an empty stomach; a famine-stricken man gains consolation from no creed." Soldiers did not so much reject religion as exhaust its ability to explain what was happening to them. Many Southern soldiers grew weary of preachers' promises and retreated once again into their battle-hardened shell, convinced they had suffered enough in this war. As Hunter put it, "They had such a hell of a time in this country that the good Lord would not see them damned in the next." Others, convinced they had suffered far too much, gave up on the Southern cause and deserted.

Confederate troops found a number of compelling reasons for deserting. Soldiers might conclude that the Confederacy had abandoned them first: rations were chronically inadequate and were periodically reduced even further, shoes and clothing were constantly in short supply, and soldiers seldom saw a paymaster. Or they might determine that the war was hopeless. A Georgia soldier decided he had seen enough when the Confederates had to abandon Chattanooga, Tennessee, in September 1863: "There is no use fighting any longer no how, for we are done gon up the Spout."

But an especially urgent reason to desert was hardship at home. Many Southern wives were accustomed to a vital role in farming and were prepared to take over while their husbands were in the army, and others received help from neighbors and relatives. Being shorthanded, however, compounded problems that would have been overwhelming even with a husband present. Salt (an essential preservative) and other supplies ran short, causing prices to soar, and armies on both sides routinely helped themselves to the crops that families managed to raise. Wives pleaded with their husbands to return: "Before God, Edward," wrote Mary Cooper of North Carolina, "unless you come home, we must die." A Mississippi soldier, recipient of a similar plea from his family, pointed out that "we are poor men and willing to defend our country but our families [come] first."

And so men left, singly and in groups. Soldiers slipped away from camp at night, dropped out on the march, and refused to return from furloughs; an estimated 104,000 Confederates deserted during the war. Richard Reid's study of North Carolina deserters suggests the potency of home-front conditions in inspiring desertions. Desertion rates were especially high among men in their late twenties, who typically had young children at home, and among men from the northeast part of the state, the area most threatened by Union troops. Desertion was also common among the reluctant soldiers who joined in 1863 and 1864, though leaving had little to do with fear of combat: 70 percent of North Carolina deserters had served for more than a year. Bessie Martin's study of desertion among Alabama troops shows high desertion rates in poorer counties, and historian Victoria Bynum has found that belonging to female-headed households, which had been shorthanded even before the war, raised the likelihood that men in a North Carolina county would desert or evade the draft.

Confederate officials tried to stem the tide of deserters with increasingly severe punishments. As in the Union army, Con-

federates at first depended on public humiliation to deter misbehavior, including desertion. Later, however, leaders over-
came their aversion to harsh punishment and increasingly
sentenced deserters to execution. There are no Southern statistics to compare with the Union army, but Confederate authorities may have been harsher on deserters than were Union
commanders. In two multiple executions in 1864, twelve deserters were shot in Georgia and twenty-two were hanged
after being caught in Union uniforms in North Carolina. But
desertions increased right along with executions, and by 1865
the Confederate army had more men absent (most of them
without leave) than were present for duty.

Indeed, the Confederacy had only 160,000 "effectives" in
early 1865, and the number was dwindling rapidly. Why did
anyone remain in the army under these circumstances? The
South had no reenlistment crisis comparable to the Union's in
1864, because in February its Congress simply extended the
terms of three-year men. This act surely encouraged more desertions, but a number of soldiers also took part in symbolic
"reenlistments" to raise morale (and to earn furloughs). Simple duty and patriotism explain much of soldiers' persever-
ance: a Confederate general, for example, felt "honor bound
to fight to the bitter end, unless authorities should direct
otherwise."

Yet there were other motives woven into patriotic sentiments. In a North Carolina study, desertion rates were especially *low* among merchants, professionals such as physicians
and lawyers, and men from slaveholding areas; deserters were
likewise uncommon among slaveholders in Alabama and in a
regiment from Virginia's "black belt." Men from the Southern
gentry undoubtedly fought on because they could not bear the
destruction of their society—an ordered society with proper-
tied gentlemen at the top, setting an example of leadership for

all white men. Yankees promised to take away their property and their right to lead, and to make blacks equal with whites—a society not worth living in. Other soldiers found their loyalty to state and country mixed with loyalty to comrades. Deserting a doomed cause was one thing, but abandoning comrades, the only people who truly understood what soldiers had endured, was unthinkable. And so men made agonizing choices between conflicting ways of surviving, conflicting duties, and conflicting loyalties.

The Confederate armies that surrendered in the spring of 1865 were a shadow of their former strength. Four regiments of the Army of Tennessee, for example, had once numbered more than 1,000 men each; when they surrendered in North Carolina in late April the four regiments amounted to 179 ragged soldiers. They and other Confederates turned in most of their weapons, signed an oath of allegiance to the federal government, and made their way home as best they could. Where possible they took riverboats or railroads, but most Southern transportation had been wrecked during the war; many officers still had their horses, but the majority of ex-soldiers had to walk home, begging for food or breaking into army storehouses as they went. Sixty thousand Confederates were also released from Northern prisons and awaited transportation southward.

5

Union Veterans in Postwar America

UNION SOLDIERS WERE still in the army even though the fighting was over. The federal government intended to demobilize most of the million remaining soldiers, but they would have to be assembled in places where their discharge records could be processed and they could be paid. The two main armies—the Army of the Potomac and Sherman's Army of Georgia—were to go to Washington, D.C., and then to their original mustering-in camps, after first marching in a mass parade in the capital.

Northern soldiers also had to endure one more shock—the assassination of Abraham Lincoln on April 14, 1865. The shooting enraged Union troops and led to reprisals against Confederates, but commanders controlled vengeful soldiers until they again turned their attention homeward. Sherman's army had much the longer journey to Washington, and officers, competing to be the first to complete the trip, drove their exhausted men northward in some of the most grueling marches of the war.

Union soldiers were ambivalent about going home. Although they had continued to revere their own homes and families even as they became alienated from the home front in general, two worries nagged at soldiers when going home became a reality. They feared that the war had changed them too much. Charles Willis of Illinois suspected that his army experience "unfits me for civil life. . . . I have almost a dread of being a citizen, of trying to be sharp, and trying to make money." Willis was certain that "citizens are not like soldiers." Going out into this alien world created another dilemma— leaving the only people who truly knew what a soldier's life was. Sergeant Richard Reeves, for one, admitted that "it seemed like breaking up a family to separate."

In the armies marching to Washington, some soldiers were also less than thrilled about the Grand Review in the capital. "We are tired & sick of Reviews already & never wish to see another as long as we live," wrote a Connecticut soldier, and another called the parade "our grand foolery." But these were young men who had just saved the Union; they did not mean to let a few misgivings and some formalities prevent them from resuming their lives.

The Grand Review was a panorama of the Union military experience. Like the army, it was enormous—200,000 troops marched down Pennsylvania Avenue on May 23 and 24, 1865. The parade also reflected regional differences within the army. Habits of self-control had made their greatest inroads in the Northeastern states, and the greatest admirers of discipline in the army were Easterners, from New Yorker George Mc-Clellan to Eastern enlisted men. Westerners were more inclined, as an Eastern soldier complained, to "laxity of discipline and personal appearances." The animosity continued after the Confederate surrender, as Eastern and Western soldiers got into brawls on the march to Washington.

In the Grand Review the predominantly Eastern Army of the Potomac marched on May 23 in new uniforms with polished brass and white dress gloves. The next day Sherman's soldiers, nearly half of whom were Westerners, showed their disdain for discipline. They paraded past the president and other high officials much as they had marched through Georgia—in shabby uniforms and ruined shoes, carrying some of their booty, including cattle, live chickens, a litter of pigs, and a goat. According to an observer, Sherman's men "chatted, laughed and cheered, just as they pleased, all along the route of the march."

The Review also reflected the army's official view of the war as a white men's crusade. During the war both armies represented in the Review had included African-American troops, but only a few black soldiers (employed as teamsters or manual laborers) appeared in the parade. Official discomfort over the exemplary contribution of black troops would endure for decades.

The War Department found another role for black soldiers that it thought was more appropriate than marching in parades. Recognizing that most whites would probably refuse to serve past the end of the war, and believing that soldiers' rations and pay would help men who had recently been slaves, federal officials decided to keep large numbers of black troops in the army for duty in the South. While white soldiers were collecting their pay and making final preparations to go home, black troops were on their way to the land from which many had escaped. The troops were to keep the peace and to assist the recently created Freedmen's Bureau in protecting ex-slaves' rights. Most black soldiers were still under the direction of white officers; the few African Americans who served as officers during and after the war were primarily surgeons and chaplains.

Black soldiers were sometimes successful in their new assignment: an observer in the South noted that "when colored Soldiers are about [whites] are afraid to kick colored women and abuse colored people in the Streets, as they usually do." But

black soldiers were just as often unable even to protect themselves against resentful Southerners. White gangs assaulted
and murdered black troops in a number of Southern towns, a
Virginia resident tried to poison a black unit's well, and some
South Carolinians ambushed a train carrying a black regiment.

Under these conditions, signs of strain appeared between
black enlisted men and white officers. Chafing at peacetime
duty, officers occasionally vented their frustration by harshly
punishing their men, and the troops sometimes fought back.
One black regiment forcibly freed some of its members from
punishment, and another group of soldiers exchanged gunfire
with its officers after a dispute over discipline. The mutinies
were put down and the participants imprisoned or executed,
but the incidents show that black soldiers had become
schooled in activism as well as in warfare. An observer noted
that "no negro who has ever been a soldier can again be imposed upon; they have learnt what it is to be free and they will
infuse their feelings into others." Indeed, a significant number
of Union army veterans were among the African Americans
who became legislators and members of Congress while the
Republican party controlled Southern states in the late 1860s
and early 1870s.

Eventually black units were demobilized, but ex-soldiers
were hardly safe from whites' wrath. In May 1866 a white
mob in Memphis attacked newly discharged soldiers, killing
forty-six and injuring more than seventy others. And if they
went north, African-American veterans could anticipate hostility from Northern whites.

Black veterans, however, were not the only soldiers who
faced a suspicious Northern society: civilians were as ambivalent about veterans as the soldiers had been about coming
home. Civilians were glad that the war was over, but they
feared the worst from men who had been living by the dic-

tates of war rather than the rules of civilization. The author Nathaniel Hawthorne worried that "when the soldiers returned the quiet rural life of the New England villages would be spoiled and coarsened," and a newspaper editor acknowledged "the belief that the army has acted as a school of demoralization."

Returning soldiers provided some evidence for these fears. Ex-soldiers looted and brawled in New York, Washington, and elsewhere in the summer of 1865; former soldiers, upset at being denied a promised bonus, went on an arson spree in Madison, Wisconsin, in 1866. Prison officials across the country reported a sharp increase in inmates, asserted that most of them were ex-soldiers, and blamed army life for the crime wave. Historians have generally agreed that the war corrupted soldiers and thus contributed to postwar crime. A more complete look at the evidence undermines this explanation. Crime did increase after the war, but the country experienced crime waves in the 1850s and during the war as well. The homicide rate, which should reflect the activities of army-trained killers, steadily *fell* after the war and showed a steep rise only in 1870 before falling again. Indeed, the sharpest rise in all crimes occurred in 1870. Why criminal tendencies bred by military service would have revealed themselves in a single outburst five years after Appomattox is difficult to explain. Also of note is that many crimes following demobilization were *against* soldiers: thieves and swindlers often descended on soldiers' discharge points, robbing and fleecing veterans of their mustering-out pay.

A problem that lasted longer was soldiers' addiction to drugs and alcohol. Army surgeons' sympathy for suffering patients had led them to dispense morphine freely, creating an addiction in many of the recipients. After the war, physicians gave additional morphine to already addicted veterans and introduced others to the drug in order to treat the lingering pain of wounds (and occasionally to relieve the aftereffects of combat stress). There were numerous civilian addicts as well, but morphine dependency nonetheless became known as "the army disease," and in 1879 an army surgeon estimated that 45,000 veterans were addicted to morphine.

Public misgivings about the character of returning Union soldiers thus had some basis, but they were nevertheless exaggerated. Criminals and addicts were a small fraction of the roughly 1.5 million Union soldiers who survived the war and had not deserted the army. Yet even men who returned without criminal tendencies or addiction encountered a mixed reception. Evidence indicates that if they were white, and if they reached home soon enough, veterans at least found employment. Rhode Island took a census in June 1865, when about half its soldiers were back from the war—some discharged during the war for disability or expired enlistments, plus the first men mustered out following the surrender. In a sample of men from this census, there are no appreciable differences between the occupations of white veterans and civilians.

The fortunes of African Americans, however, were different. Black veterans in Rhode Island were four times as likely to be unemployed as were white *veterans*, and five times as likely to be jobless as black *civilians*. White soldiers who were discharged early enough could find work in the vigorous wartime economy, but black men were closed out of most occupations that benefited from war production. When a black veteran came to Providence or Newport, he had to compete with other African Americans for whatever work became available for porters, day laborers, or other unskilled workers.

Veterans who came home later in 1865, whether they were black or white, had a more difficult time. Roughly 300,000 soldiers were discharged each month at the height of demobilization in mid-1965, and by the year's end nearly a million men had been released. Information comparable to the Rhode Island census is unavailable for these later returnees, but there is evidence that increasing numbers of veterans were going jobless. Situation-wanted advertisements began appearing in newspapers, and the United States Sanitary Commission, which had assisted in medical care during the war, opened employment bureaus to place veterans in jobs. In New York, veterans formed their own employment agency. Yet veterans poured into the cities faster than jobs opened. In August 250 veterans staged a march in New York, with banners proclaiming "Looking for Bread & Work," and the following winter a city official reported seeing several hundred veterans, "homeless, houseless, and hungry," with "no food, save the cold victuals obtained by begging."

This crisis passed; employment became available for some of the seekers, while others traveled west and south, taking work as farmhands, teamsters, miners, or whatever else they could find. We must remember that the North was still largely rural. Many discharged soldiers shared the experience of Lieutenant Leander Stillwell, who hitched a wagon ride from the train station and then walked the last nine miles to his parents' farm in Illinois. The next day Stillwell was out cutting corn, feeling "as if I had been away only a day or two, and had just taken up the farm work where I had left off."

But trouble could still develop for soldiers who returned to home and family. There is evidence of a high postwar divorce rate among officers who had served with the U.S. Colored Troops, and some states likewise showed a sharp rise in divorces, led by Ohio's 40 percent increase from 1865 to 1866. On the other hand, as usually happens after a war, most states also recorded an increase in marriages—Ohio, for example, had nearly a 40 percent increase in the number of marriages in the same year.

Veterans' joblessness and psychological problems eventually aroused considerable sympathy—newspapers in the first year after the war carried numerous descriptions of destitute ex-soldiers and described veterans' suicides—but these troubles by themselves inspired little government action. Many veterans did, however, have a problem that was widely recognized as deserving of public help—physical disability. More than 200,000 soldiers had returned with wounds, and many other veterans continued to suffer from diseases they contracted in the army, from chronic diarrhea to tuberculosis. It had long been a principle of American government that disabled veterans were entitled to public aid, and Abraham Lincoln had underscored the commitment with a promise "to care for him who shall have borne the battle." To fulfill this obligation, the federal government expanded on the two customary methods of caring for disabled soldiers.

Pensions were the usual form of compensation for war wounds. Poor and disabled veterans from previous wars had received pensions, and in 1862 Congress authorized pensions for Union soldiers. A veteran could receive $8 to $30 a month, depending on rank, for "total disability" incurred in the line of duty (or a portion of these amounts for partial disability), and soldiers' widows could also qualify for a pension. Lawmakers soon began to amend the payment provisions, adding new categories of payment for specific disabilities such as loss of a hand, loss of a foot, loss of a hand *and* a foot, and so on. Applying for a pension could be cumbersome (if a soldier's disability was not obvious, for example, a physician would have to verify it), and many veterans were unaware of pensions, so relatively few ex-soldiers applied at first. Fewer than 10 percent of

Union veterans were on the pension rolls through the 1860s and 1870s.

A change in the law in 1879, however, dramatically opened up the pension system. Until then, payments began when a claim was approved by the Pension Bureau, and were dated from the time of application and not from the soldier's discharge (or his death, in the case of a widow). For example, a soldier who learned about pensions in 1875 and had a claim approved the next year would receive nothing for the ten years he had been out of the army. Pensions that were retroactive to the date of discharge or death would attract thousands of new applicants, a fact understood by pension attorneys and claims agents. These individuals assisted veterans and widows in submitting applications in exchange for a fee, and they led a campaign for retroactive pensions in the late 1870s. Although pension attorneys were roundly detested as "the worst class of vermin that ever infested the body-politic," politicians of both parties were intrigued by the voting power represented by disabled veterans. Republicans sought to solidify the loyalty of ex-soldiers to the party of Abraham Lincoln, and Democrats, restored to national potency after the readmission of Southern states to the Union, wished to affirm their own patriotism. As a result, Northern members of Congress voted almost unanimously for the "arrears bill" of 1879, which authorized lump-sum retroactive payments to current pensioners and those filing new claims before mid-1880. The retroactive payments averaged roughly $1,000, and veterans filed more than nine thousand new claims a month in 1879 and 1880, versus about sixteen hundred a month previously; the proportion of veterans who were on the pension rolls more than doubled during the 1880s.

Yet even a generous pension system could not meet the needs of all disabled veterans. Federal officials had for some time recognized that some veterans were homeless or so disabled that they required institutional care; before the Civil War the government had operated homes for soldiers and sailors who were disabled or had served at least twenty years. Local governments and charities, including the Sanitary Commission, operated shelters for needy soldiers during the Civil War, and by war's end a number of politicians, business leaders, and social reformers were calling for a permanent asylum for volunteer soldiers. One advocate insisted that disabled ex-soldiers "should have a nation's gratitude, a nation's care, and a place in the nation's household, a seat by the nation's fireside." Congress agreed, and in March 1865 it authorized creation of a national asylum for Union veterans. By the end of 1870 branches had opened in Maine, Ohio, Wisconsin, and Virginia, and had admitted more than 3,200 ex-soldiers. About 1,400 veterans entered the homes each year in the 1870s and early 1880s; when old age was classified as a disability after 1884, yearly admissions nearly doubled, and more branch homes were added to the system. A number of Northern states established their own soldiers' homes in the 1880s, and some admitted soldiers' wives and widows as well as the veterans themselves.

Ex-soldiers applied in person or in writing to the homes, and were admitted, if space was available, when the management had verified their service record and, in the early decades, determined that their disability was war-related. The homes furnished barracks for sleeping quarters and provided residents with medical care, food, uniforms, and other supplies. The men spent their time tending their institution's farm, reading in the library, working in the laundry or blacksmith shop, or, in the early years, taking classes. They could leave the institution when they felt able and could return with permission.

But this was not a carefree life. Government officials were as wary of ex-soldiers as was the rest of society. The Sanitary Commission, which initially had been skeptical of soldiers' homes, warned that the institutions would fill up with "foreigners, the reckless and unrelated, those who have hitherto been afloat, . . . or [those who] have least natural force to provide for themselves." Even though veterans' advocates tried to differentiate ex-soldiers from inmates of poorhouses, they could not help viewing veterans as akin to other nineteenth-century dependent groups who were generally assumed to be suffering from a moral weakness that could be cured by instilling self-discipline. Since ex-soldiers were already familiar with army discipline, the ideal policy for soldiers' homes was to give them more of it. The only way the homes would work, the Sanitary Commission believed, was to make them "military in their organization, control, dress, [and] drill." Residents thus arose to reveille, ate at mess tables, were organized into companies, and were given furloughs and honorable or dishonorable discharges.

But many residents of soldiers' homes did not consider themselves to be military men—they were civilians who had had their health ruined while fighting for the common good. Union soldiers had grudgingly tolerated military discipline in time of war, but they were unlikely to accept the same regimentation to please a staff of administrators. A chaplain at the home in Dayton, Ohio, explained the residents' attitude: "They want to forget the past. Their series of affliction, the breaking up of their families, and their mental and physical disabilities, put them in a position which causes them to absolutely hate anything military. . . . They feel that military discipline is irksome."

As a result, residents often resisted the homes' discipline, in ways that ranged from trivial defiance to outright challenge.

They stole from the kitchen, missed roll calls, and got drunk, which annoyed the managers, and they protested the handling of pensions, which made management furious. Soldiers' homes often withheld part or all of the payments due to resident pensioners, seeing the policy as essential to proper discipline. According to one home's managers, "as soon as they receive their quarterly payments [many residents] go outside and spend it all on drink." Residents often saw it otherwise. They believed they had earned their pensions just as they had earned admittance to a soldiers' home, and the managers had no right to take their money.

Residents thus protested individually and in groups: in Maine in 1869 and Pennsylvania in 1891, sizable groups of residents walked out to protest pension withholding, and the managers of the Wisconsin state home declared that "no one thing during the life of the Home has done so much to create friction among the members and cause them to become dissatisfied" as had the pension issue. Indeed, samples of federal and state soldiers' home residents from the 1880s and 1890s show that the higher a veteran's pension, the more likely he was to leave after only a few months in a home. Managers did keep the upper hand: they could hand out punishments ranging from revocation of furlough privileges to a dishonorable discharge, so order prevailed in the homes. The cost, however, was bitterness among residents—John Garrigan, at the Dayton federal home, reported that "often I wish I was in the penitentiary [or] that I was hanged or dead"—and undoubted hardships for many of those who left the homes in protest.

Although veterans vigorously defended their entitlement to public compensation for their disabilities, they also tried to deal with misfortune through a revival of their wartime comradeship. In addition to individual efforts to help fellow veterans obtain work, veterans tried to organize for companionship and mutual aid. Most of these groups were short-lived, except for the Grand Army of the Republic, founded in Illinois in 1866. The GAR combined military forms (annual meetings were encampments, misbehavior was adjudicated by courts-martial, and meetings were guarded by sentries, for example) and the secret rituals of fraternal orders like the Masons and the Odd Fellows. As Stuart McConnell points out in his study of the Grand Army, the founders hoped to line up soldier-voters behind Republican candidates and to keep alive the army spirit of mutual aid; veterans themselves also saw meetings as ideal occasions for socializing. Soon after the GAR's founding, local "posts" sprang up around the country, but interest in the organization dwindled by the end of the 1860s. After a brief period of interest in the war, Americans settled into a decade in which they were more anxious to forget the conflict than to relive it, thus dampening interest in veterans' groups. The GAR hurt its own cause by introducing a system of membership ranks that offended members who believed that wartime ranks were distinction enough among veterans. The order's national membership languished at about thirty thousand through most of the 1870s.

But the Grand Army underwent an extraordinary revival in the 1880s. Civilians rekindled their interest in literature and observances having to do with the Civil War; and the GAR made itself more accessible by dropping some of the more painful Civil War symbolism (a prisoner-of-war blanket, for example, and a firing-squad reenactment) and emphasizing instead a spirit of fraternity among members. Although the GAR had had little to do with passage of the Arrears Act of 1879, the act itself stimulated interest in veterans' groups. Spurred by these developments, membership in the GAR rebounded dramatically, to 60,000 in 1880, 270,000 in 1885, and to a peak in 1890 at more than 400,000 members.

Other veterans' groups arose in the 1880s, but they were more exclusive than the GAR (for example, the Union Veteran Legion limited its membership to veterans who had served for at least two years or been wounded) or were single-issue lobbying groups (such as the Service Pension Association). The composition of GAR posts generally reflected the men in their communities. Some urban posts drew from the business community and charged high dues and "muster fees"; their membership thus consisted largely of professionals and merchants who belonged to—or clerks and bookkeepers who wanted to belong to—the commercial elite. Posts in working-class or rural areas, on the other hand, contained large numbers of manual laborers or farmers, and charged lower dues and fees. Even these posts tended to select local business leaders as officers (for example, post commander or adjutant), and working-class posts seldom took a position on labor issues.

The GAR engaged in a variety of activities. Its meetings, from post gatherings to state and national encampments, were valued chances for socializing. The author Hamlin Garland's father would not dream of missing a post meeting, and at a national encampment "he was like a boy on Circus Day." Charity for needy comrades was also central to the Grand Army. Funds raised through fees and donations bought food, paid the rent, and covered the funeral expenses of destitute veterans and widows, and members provided in-kind benefits such as medical care to comrades in need. GAR men also gave preference to members in hiring or in patronizing businesses, and the organization was instrumental in convincing states to fund veterans' pensions and soldiers' homes.

The Grand Army also served as a disseminator of self-control. Ideal GAR members were, according to a founder, "trained, drilled and disciplined gentlemen," though sometimes this ideal had to be enforced. Drunkenness, that cardinal loss of self-control, was also the most common infraction brought before courts-martial. Members of a court-martial could hand down punishments that included censure and dishonorable discharge. Courts-martial were infrequent, but they demonstrated prominent Union veterans' continuing concern with order and self-control—qualities they believed were lacking in civilian society and must be promoted that much more vigorously among the men who had preserved the Union.

The GAR was, however, noticeably uncomfortable with some of the nation's saviors. Some Northern posts had a few African-American members, but black leadership over white veterans was unthinkable; separate black and white posts were the rule where black veterans were numerous. The South also had GAR posts to serve the substantial population of Union veterans who had moved there after the war. These posts were especially hostile to black veterans, and their virtually all-white membership went unchallenged until the late 1880s. When black veterans tried to organize Southern posts, white Southerners first refused to charter them and then insisted on separate "departments" (administrative units of one or more states) to avoid any chance of African Americans commanding whites. The national leadership rejected this segregation but was unable to enforce its decision; Southern members maintained segregated departments. In the 1890s the attitude of the GAR's leaders was largely the attitude of soldiers during the war—they condemned the grosser forms of racial oppression but were unwilling to make a priority of ending them.

The order's views on women were similar. George Lemon, a Washington pension attorney and unofficial GAR spokesman, published a number of endorsements of women's rights in his weekly newspaper, the *National Tribune*. Lemon condemned wife abuse, called for more egalitarian marriages, and cheered the admission of women to practice as lawyers. But within the GAR, women were expected to be the same faithful supporters they had been during the war—to raise funds, make flags, serve food, and otherwise sustain their men. The Grand Army established a Woman's Relief Corps in 1881 to allow women to perform these duties while remaining safely separate from and subordinate to the main organization.

The GAR's most notorious activity was its pension lobbying. The Arrears Act of 1879, in addition to encouraging a flurry of pension applications, also sorted out the key actors in the emerging pension debate. Lemon and his fellow pension attorneys could be counted on for enthusiastic support of anything that would increase applications. Among politicians, Republicans most consistently cast their lot with veterans: Republicans represented Lincoln's party, and they realized that Democrats' current insistence on governmental cost-cutting could be portrayed as meanness directed at ex-soldiers.

And veterans' leaders, invigorated by the GAR's growth, underwent a change of philosophy. In the organization's early years, leaders had essentially agreed with the basis of pension law—that pensions were compensation for disabilities caused by service to the government, and that veterans' life after the war was a separate existence. In the 1880s, however, leading veterans' spokesmen changed their view—now it was once a soldier, always a soldier. Some veterans' advocates pressed for a pension for all disabled ex-soldiers, whether or not the disability had been incurred in the war; others went even further and demanded a "service" pension, a payment to all ex-soldiers and widows simply for the men's service to their country. A universal service pension could not draw enough congressional support to pass, so pension advocates set their sights on what became known as a "dependent" pension, since disabled veterans depended on someone else for support. In 1887 Congress passed a dependent pension bill, providing for a $12 pension per month for fully disabled Union veterans, and sent it to President Grover Cleveland, a Democrat.

Cleveland, viewing the bill as an administrative nightmare and a raid on the federal treasury, vetoed it. Veterans' advocates already detested the president for having hired a substitute in the war, and when Cleveland tried to return captured Confederate flags later in 1887, leading veterans made a crusade of unseating him at the next election. Republicans and veterans' spokesmen focused special attention on Indiana and New York, "swing states" in contemporary elections. "Corporal" James Tanner, a GAR official and tireless veterans' activist, concentrated on Indiana, where he boasted that he "plastered the state with promises" of pension increases under a Republican administration.

The Republicans nominated former general Benjamin Harrison for president in 1888 and promised pensions "so enlarged and extended as to provide against the possibility that any man who honorably wore the Federal uniform should become the inmate of an almshouse or dependent on private charity." Democrats, on the other hand, promised to govern by "carefully guarding the interests of the taxpayers." Cleveland won the popular vote in the election, but the distribution of the votes, including wins in New York and Indiana, gave Harrison the victory in the electoral college.

Did veterans put their comrade in the White House? It is impossible to know for certain how individuals voted, but we can estimate their behavior with reasonable accuracy. Such an estimate for the crucial state of Indiana can be made from its distribution of veterans, GAR members, and vote totals. At the time of the 1888 election, Indiana had 63,000 veterans, 24,000 of whom were GAR members. As we would expect, an estimate of GAR members' voting shows a considerable Republican majority—virtually all members turned out to vote, and they voted more than two-to-one for Harrison. Indiana veterans who did not belong to the GAR, however, voted quite differently: like noncombatants, non-GAR veterans divided evenly between Cleveland and Harrison. The political activism and soldier-first attitude of the GAR applied primarily to those who joined the order; in their voting behavior, the large number of veterans who did not join were scarcely distinguishable from the nonveteran population.

Veterans' dominance of politics reached its peak under Harrison. Congress revived the dependent pension legislation, modified it to call for a scale of payments from $6 to $12 a month depending on the degree of a veteran's disability, and sent it to the president in 1890; Harrison eagerly signed it. Veterans could now earn a pension if they were disabled for almost any reason (except from "their own vicious habits"), and widows could qualify if their husband had died from any cause. The result was a tidal wave of new applications. More than 650,000 claims were filed in the new law's first year, creating an enormous backlog of paperwork at the Pension Bureau in spite of its efforts to ease the investigation of claims.

Even before the new law had passed, Harrison named Corporal Tanner commissioner of pensions, allegedly telling him to "be liberal with the boys." Tanner's militant promises of "a pension for every old soldier who needs one" drew protests from politicians and newspaper editors and he was forced to resign, but his successor, another GAR official, was similarly generous in approving pension applications. The proportion of applications approved was higher under Harrison than it had been under Cleveland, and there is evidence that approvals under both presidents were aimed at shoring up political support. One study found that new pensions in Ohio during the Harrison administration went primarily to strong Republican areas; another study found a similar Democratic bias in Indiana in the previous Cleveland administration. By the end of Harrison's term more than 70 percent of veterans were on the pension rolls, compared with approximately 20 percent in 1885.

But Republicans had gone beyond the limits of acceptable compensation to veterans. Generosity to ex-soldiers had opponents as well as supporters, and foes became increasingly irate during the Harrison administration. Commissioner Tanner had been denounced as "a loud-mouthed Grand Army stump speaker," and a commentator decried the "indiscriminate and lavish distribution of pensions" under the Dependent Pension Act. Another pension opponent declared that "the ex-Union soldier is coming to stand in the public mind for a helpless and greedy sort of person, who says that he is not able to support himself, and whines that other people ought to do it for him." Public displeasure with the pension explosion offset veterans' loyalty to the Republican party and helped Cleveland regain the White House in 1892. Cleveland immediately moved to crack down on pension approvals: his pension commissioner cut the number of applications approved to about seven hundred a month in his first full year, compared with more than six thousand a month in Harrison's last year.

By this time the influence of veterans in presidential politics was fading. Although Congress would periodically increase pension coverage and payments, Republicans no longer made generosity to veterans the centerpiece of their platforms, and veterans' leaders no longer concentrated their energies on expanding pensions. Indeed, the GAR began to lose members in the 1890s. Although the decline was nothing like the explosive growth of the 1880s, the organization did lose nearly a third of its membership in the 1890s, reflecting a waning interest as well as the dying off of members. The Grand Army had been instrumental in making pensions available to the majority of ex-soldiers, and many saw no further need for the organization; others, however, remained in the order because it offered a way of coping with the passing of their generation.

This passing became an increasing reality for Union veterans in the 1890s. By mid-decade most ex-soldiers were in their fifties, too young to stop working (especially in a country that was just beginning to develop a concept of retirement), but old enough to have a full generation between them and the Civil War. Veterans' children had reached adulthood and most were on their own by the 1890s: 90 percent of men in their mid-fifties had no children under sixteen living with them.

And the nation was changing as ex-soldiers looked on. The United States population was becoming younger and more foreign-born as millions of immigrants came from southern and eastern Europe, and the economy was becoming increasingly dominated by huge, impersonal corporations. The growth of cities and wage employment, whose insecurity many men had tried to escape by enlisting in the 1860s, had continued beyond anyone's expectations: New York City, for example, had nearly tripled in size since 1860, and across the country the number of wage workers in manufacturing had quadrupled. Although interest in Civil War generals and battles continued through the 1890s, many veterans undoubtedly believed that the nation they had saved was becoming dangerously unrecognizable.

As they approached old age in this disturbing society, many Union veterans worried about their legacy. They believed they had made a unique contribution to the nation and had a unique responsibility to preserve their heritage. This meant more than rehashing Civil War battles; it also meant recreating the kind of nation that veterans believed they had saved—a nation characterized by order, discipline, and vigorous patriotism. This was a highly idealized version of antebellum and wartime conditions, but it was a vision that the GAR had long nurtured in its rituals and procedures.

In the 1890s the GAR focused direct attention on the veterans' legacy. The organization began a campaign to instill in schoolchildren the values it saw as essential to reviving a virtuous and orderly society. GAR leaders worked to ensure that history textbooks portrayed the Civil War as a vindication of national unity against the forces of rebellion. They insisted on making the flag a sacred icon, urging schools to use the Pledge of Allegiance and lobbying to make Flag Day a holiday, and GAR officials agitated for military drill for schoolboys. The GAR also applauded the Spanish-American War, portraying this series of one-sided engagements as a fulfillment of the Civil War's patriotic heritage.

At the same time Union veterans were also reconciling with their old adversaries: Blue-Gray battlefield reunions and memorial services had become common events by the turn of the century. Some GAR posts objected to such fraternization as a betrayal of patriotism, but the prevailing view was that, as they had during the war, soldiers on both sides continued to share a bond that could be distinguished from their causes. The *National Tribune* summarized this reasoning when it praised Confederate soldiers for their "manly daring, fortitude, and devotion to an idea (though a wrong one)."

6

Confederate Veterans in the Postwar South

THERE WERE NO grand parades for Confederate soldiers. Their army, and the government that had employed it,
ceased to exist at the surrender, and most of them had to make
their own way home. When they arrived they found changes
that added to the traumas of their army experience.

Although it may seem that no peacetime experience could
have the effect that the miseries of army life and the horrors
of combat had, we must put the war's psychological impact
into perspective. The coarsening of soldiers was real enough,
but it also had limits. James McPherson found no significant
change during the war in Union or Confederate soldiers' patriotic sentiments. And cultural historian Michael Barton,
looking for evidence of a more elemental kind of change in
soldiers' diaries, found no trends in Confederates' *identity* during the war. If soldiers had associated themselves with the
Confederacy more or less often as the war progressed, or if
they had begun to substitute "we" for "I" in personal references, we might conclude that they had indeed become fundamentally different individuals. Yet there was no variation over
time in the way they identified themselves; Confederate sol-

diers came home battle-toughened but not fundamentally altered.

But the society they rejoined was profoundly changing. Part of the change was economic: whites were confronted with a population of freedpeople they would have to employ rather than own, and struggling farmers would have to depend more than ever on cotton and on the merchants who controlled the flow of cash and credit. Part was political: Southerners would have to restructure their governments under the watchful eye of Northern authorities. And perhaps the greatest change of all was the legacy of defeat. White Southerners had long been convinced of their superiority and fiercely protective of their security, but now they were saddled with defeat and uncertainty. In the wake of the Confederate surrender, no one knew what to expect next. Punishment of the war's participants, seizure of land, reprisals by resentful Unionists and former slaves—anything was possible.

Confederate veterans, who were in a position to feel the sting of defeat more painfully than others, reacted in a number of ways. Some preached emigration and tried to start colonies in Latin America and elsewhere. Only a few thousand former Confederates left the country, however, and none of their settlements lasted very long. Other Confederates pulled up stakes for more modest moves, but most were unwilling to leave the South. When federal census-takers first identified Civil War veterans in 1890, only 7 percent of Confederates were living outside the former slave states; in contrast, liberalized land-grant policies for Union veterans encouraged them to move, and nearly 15 percent were living outside what had been the wartime Union. For Confederates, Texas was the one great magnet. Here were vast amounts of land in a former Confederate state; an Alabama woman wrote that her neighbors were "anxious to go to Texas where a great many think they can live without work." By 1890 Texas was home to more Confederate veterans than any other state, despite having been only sixth in population in the wartime Confederacy.

Many veterans, however, returned home intending to stay. In a sample of military-age men in Mississippi, nearly 40 percent of veterans who had survived the war were still in the same county in 1870 as in 1860. This may seem low, but only about 20 percent of noncombatants remained in their prewar county. Veterans may have provided much of what continuity Southern communities possessed.

But reactions to defeat were not confined to decisions about moving. Defeat was an affront to soldiers' manhood, and some Southern veterans took out their anger on civilian society. Veterans played a major role in the violence and lawlessness that erupted across the South soon after the war's end. Former soldiers ransacked Confederate army storehouses, assaulted and robbed civilians, attacked Unionists, and settled old scores with personal enemies. The provisional governor of Texas declared that "human life in Texas is not to day worth as much, so far as law or protection can give value to it, as that of domestic cattle," and in 1866 a Northern observer reported that "Mississippians have been shooting and cutting each other all over the state." Some marauders envisioned themselves as "regulators" who were punishing criminals, and outlaw bands included noncombatants as well as ex-soldiers, but much of the violence in the postwar months consisted of random aggression by defeated veterans with little to lose.

Yet most veterans did not become renegades. A more common Confederate reaction to defeat was a benumbed apathy. Southern men noticed it in themselves: Thomas Harrold of Georgia wrote that "it sometimes appears to me as if my vitality and energy were all gone." Women noticed it: Ella

Thomas, also of Georgia, remarked that her husband, a former cavalry officer, was "cast down, utterly spirit broken," and Kate Stone of Louisiana observed that her recently returned brother "rarely talks at all" and "seems to take little interest in hearing others." And freedpeople noticed it: an ex-slave from Alabama recalled that ex-soldiers were "all lookin' sick. De sperrit dey lef' wid jus' been done whupped outen dem."

This apathy was especially evident in the first postwar elections. In 1865 Southern states rewrote their constitutions to reflect the demise of slavery and the Confederacy, and voters chose state and local officials for postwar governments. Elections before the war had drawn considerable interest, and turnouts of three-quarters or more of white men were common. The elections of 1865, however, attracted fewer than half as many Southern voters as had the elections of 1860. Southern apathy toward politics was widespread, but there is evidence that Confederate veterans were particularly disinterested. The Mississippi town of Kosciusko, for example, held an election for local officials in December 1865 and left behind a list of voters. The town had 98 white men, nearly half of whom were Confederate veterans, but only three of the twelve candidates for office were ex-soldiers. Four in ten nonveterans voted in the election, a turnout that was in line with overall Southern figures, but fewer than three in ten veterans bothered to vote, and only one veteran was elected to office.

Veterans played a more complex role in statewide politics. Historians have noted that most of the men elected in 1865 and 1866 had been political moderates in 1861, and had opposed secession. But many of them were also former Confederate soldiers or government officials who had cast their lot with the South in spite of their views. Among those elected to take seats in Congress, presuming their states were to be readmitted, were ten former Confederate generals and the Confederate vice-president. Were voters thus seeking to continue the Civil War on the legislative front?

Evidence from Mississippi suggests that voters in 1865 looked for leadership rather than simple Confederate patriotism. In races for state representative where voters had a choice between veterans and nonveterans, being an ex-soldier made little difference in a candidate's chances of winning. On the other hand, if the candidate had been a Confederate *officer*, his chances of winning a seat were three times those of other candidates. Having exceptional wealth or a professional occupation, the traditional paths to community leadership, likewise tripled a candidate's chances of being elected. Confederate veterans actually made the contests for the Mississippi House more "democratic" than they had been before the war: a number of veterans of modest means ignored the climate of apathy and entered the races, hoping their service would commend them to the voters. But in this period of confusion and insecurity, voters were more interested in tangible credentials for leadership than in simple patriotism.

The problems of most Confederate veterans were worlds apart from the concerns of winning an election. At least 200,000 Confederate soldiers had been wounded in the war, and thousands of them had endured amputations. Disabled soldiers returned to communities that had few resources to assist them, and the aid that ex-soldiers did receive was sporadic and short-lived. During the war most Southern state governments had supplemented local aid for disabled soldiers and their families, and some states continued public assistance afterward. Arkansas, for example, set aside 10 percent of its revenues for artificial limbs and other aid to veterans and their survivors, and Georgia paid the tuition of veterans attending public colleges. Private charities also distributed food and supplies to needy Southerners, and ex-soldiers and their survivors were among the thousands of whites who received food, clothing, and other aid from the federal Freedman's Bureau. In addition, Louisiana established a soldiers' home in 1866 with a $20,000 appropriation, and the home took in nearly a hundred veterans by 1867. But these efforts would soon come to an end.

Even if they escaped war wounds and postwar poverty, many ex-soldiers encountered domestic troubles. Southern statistics are sketchy for the immediate postwar years, but diaries and letters furnish ample evidence of marital discord, abandonment, and divorce, all of which were undoubtedly aggravated by Confederate defeat and the breakdown of the Southern economy. On the other hand, the war also created a marriage boom that overshadowed the increase in marriages that occurred in the North. Since a much larger proportion of Southerners served in the army, more Southern marriages were postponed during the war, and the killing left proportionally more widows than in the North. The consequences can be seen in Alabama counties that kept good records: marriages per thousand of population increased by nearly 50 percent in the late 1860s compared with the 1860 rate. Among Northern states with usable records, the increase was only about half as great.

The Southern marriage boom indicates that postwar despondency had its limits. In times of widespread stress, young people typically postpone marrying; it is estimated, for example, that 800,000 marriages were put off during the Great Depression of the 1930s. The willingness of Southerners to marry (and to remarry, in the case of war widows) suggests that Southern apathy was largely confined to political matters. Southern men, a large percentage of whom were Confederate veterans, were willing to start a marriage amid the uncertainty of the postwar South even if they saw little point in going to the polls to choose among politicians.

One way in which Southerners could overcome their lethargy was to commemorate the Confederate dead. Memorial Day, as a springtime service for deceased soldiers, originated in the South in 1866, and numerous Southern towns began to build monuments to their fallen soldiers. Most of the monuments built before 1885 were funereal in form—simple obelisks were preferred, occasionally topped by an urn or other funeral symbol—and were located in cemeteries. Though women did much of the fund-raising and supervised the construction of the monuments, local businessmen and professionals usually organized monument societies. Many, if not most, of these men were veterans or the fathers of Confederate soldiers.

Prominent veterans also stepped to the forefront on Memorial Day and at the dedication of monuments, and their speeches were frequently a call to overcome Southern apathy. In a speech delivered in 1869, for example, a Georgian exhorted listeners to "look away from the gloom of political bondage, and fix our vision upon a coming day of triumph" when Southern principles would again prevail. The ceremonies were usually well attended, and their main purpose was the closing of wounds left open by the war.

Politicians were less willing to admit defeat. As we have seen, the representatives Southerners chose had been reluctant Confederates, but they proved equally unwilling to turn their backs on the social order of the Old South. The constitutional conventions of 1865 only grudgingly renounced slavery and secession, and the new state legislatures devoted themselves, in the words of a Republican critic, to "getting things back as near to slavery as possible." The "Black Codes" that were meant to reimpose subservience among African Americans varied from state to state, but they were based on a common set of tactics. The codes sought to bind African Americans to farm labor and to their employers by requiring blacks to sign labor contracts and discouraging employers from recruiting each other's workers. The new laws also discouraged blacks from hopes of equality with whites. Courts could seize black children, for example, on the pretext of inadequate parental support and force them into unpaid labor for white employers. The codes also stiffened penalties for theft, a charge for which conviction was usually automatic for blacks. Convicts could be whipped or sentenced to virtual enslavement to any white who paid their fine.

News of the Black Codes provoked a storm of protest from Northerners who believed the South was flouting the principles vindicated by the war. Worse yet, in the eyes of Radical Republicans who were the codes' chief critics, was President Andrew Johnson's endorsement of this defiance. Many moderate Republicans came to share the Radicals' views, and the party began to use its commanding majority in Congress to overturn the Southern policies. In 1866, over Johnson's vetoes, Congress strengthened the Freedman's Bureau and enacted the nation's first civil rights law, and sent to the states a Fourteenth Amendment that would put guarantees of equal protection and due process of law into the Constitution. In 1867, again over Johnson's vetoes, Congress required Southern states (except Tennessee, which had already been readmitted) to ratify the Fourteenth Amendment and adopt new constitutions guaranteeing the right to vote for black men; federal military commanders would supervise compliance. By 1870 the ten remaining ex-Confederate states had met these terms and been readmitted to the Union.

Under the new Southern governments, most of which were dominated by white and African-American Republicans, aid to ex-soldiers came to an end. This was not because Republican governments were particularly vindictive toward former Confederates. Relatively few ex-Confederate soldiers, for example, were barred from voting under the newly adopted constitutions. But neither were Republican officials anxious to provide public aid to men and their families who were linked to the recent fight to preserve slavery. As a result, most public assistance for Confederate veterans, such as state aid to destitute ex-soldiers and the Louisiana soldiers' home, was discontinued in the late 1860s; the Freedmen's Bureau had already begun to phase out its relief efforts in 1866.

Yet even before Republican governments came to power, some veterans had begun to put their own stamp on postwar Southern society. We have seen that Southerners, including many veterans, found comfort in laying the Confederacy to rest by commemorating fallen soldiers, but other veterans could not bear so passive an acceptance of defeat. As a result, many ex-soldiers joined, and profoundly influenced the nature of, the Ku Klux Klan.

The Klan was founded in 1866 in south-central Tennessee by six ex-Confederate soldiers, and functioned for a time as a social fraternity. Soon, however, whites in surrounding areas realized that the Klan's secrecy and practical joking could be useful in preserving white supremacy. In 1867 the original founders called interested parties to Nashville to organize an "Empire" of Klan dens under former Confederate general Nathan Bedford Forrest as Grand Wizard. In the next year the Klan adopted a credo, which in addition to affirmations of justice and patriotism pledged Klansmen to help Confederate widows and orphans. In practice the hierarchy had almost no control over local dens, and Klansmen did little to help Confederate survivors, but the importance of the Confederate war experience in the Klan's formation is clear.

The Klan that spread across the South in 1868 grew from several roots. Participating in slave patrols had been a custom (and sometimes an obligation) among white men in the antebellum South. Patrollers typically rode at night, ostensibly to enforce slave curfews, but on occasion, wearing costumes meant to frighten their victims, patrollers harassed slaves for sport. The Klan also drew on the European custom of *charivari*, a raucous festival during which disguised crowds ridiculed and assaulted adulterers, people suspected of fornication, and other wrongdoers. And the Klan clearly grew out of the traditions of frontier justice and the lynch mob.

But no influence on the Klan outweighed that of Confederate military service. Contemporary observers and later historians alike remarked on the sheer number of ex-Confederates in the Klan, especially among its leaders. This was due in part simply to the number of ex-soldiers in Southern communities, but numbers suggest only part of the significance of the Confederate experience. A network of former officers, for example, helped to spread the Klan from place to place. The local gentry who made up most of the Confederate officer corps had met men in the army whom they would not otherwise have known, and on visits and in correspondence they spread knowledge and approval of the Klan.

The war produced other motivations for joining the Klan. After the surrender, Randolph Shotwell returned to his home in western North Carolina. Shotwell knew about wartime boredom, having spent time in a Northern prison, but he nonetheless found the "dull, newsless, lifeless monotony of a village" to be "about unendurable." The Klan, however, offered him something akin to the army experience—companionship, excitement, and another chance to resist what he and his friends saw as Northern oppression, this time in the form of Republican governments. Impelled by these attractions (and, by Shotwell's admission, by liberal doses of liquor), he entered the Klan. Many other veterans undoubtedly joined for similar reasons.

The Klan's early pranks and harassment of African Americans turned into increasingly brutal terrorism against blacks' attempts at self-reliance and against the new Republican governments. Bands of Klansmen rode through Southern towns and countryside, assaulting people they saw as a political or social threat. Klansmen burned homes, churches, and schools, and whipped, tortured, mutilated, and lynched many of their victims. Klansmen's raids were not always secret: they were known to hijack trains in order to corner a victim, and local dens might band together for a major operation. In the largest such raid, an estimated five hundred Klansmen descended on Union, South Carolina, in February 1871. The raiders ordered residents off the streets, seized the jail, and lynched ten black prisoners.

The Enforcement Acts, a series of federal laws passed in 1870 and 1871, finally drove the Klan out of operation. Yet the Klan's terrorism, especially in the deep South, had already undermined Republican governments and contributed to their eventual downfall.

And the Klan never lost its connections to the Civil War. It remained largely a veterans' movement, determined to exorcise the pain of defeat as well as to terrorize its victims. A raid on a Klan den by Arkansas officials, for example, found a Confederate flag on an altar. Klansmen, especially in the group's early days, were fond of declaring to their victims that they were ghosts of the Confederate dead, returned for revenge. In contrast to the farcical militarism of antebellum militiamen, Klansmen aggressively exhibited their military prowess. Klan members staged occasional parades in town squares, complete with precision military drills, and when blacks attempted armed resistance they were often routed by battlefield-style assaults or well-coordinated sieges. Lynchings were sometimes carried out by a Klan firing squad, and Klansmen made a point of forcing the registration of Confederate veterans in places where they were barred from voting.

The Klan resembled the army in yet another way. Military leaders are obligated to take the long view—to consider strategic goals and devise tactics to achieve them. Enlisted men, however, have more immediate concerns—above all, survival with the least possible misery. The Ku Klux Klan's leaders likewise had long-term goals of crippling the Republican party in the South and eliminating Northern intervention in Southern politics. As a result, the planters, physicians, newspaper editors, and occasional minister who led the Klan tried to concentrate on political terror. Political activity, to be sure, was broadly defined: running for office as a Republican was sure to bring a visit in places where the Klan was active, but Klan leaders also ordered attacks on anyone who encouraged black self-sufficiency, from teachers to preachers to merchants who were liberal with credit for freedpeople.

Poorer whites took part in these assaults, but they also went on their own raids, intent on punishing social deviants, white and black (although Republican sympathies always increased the chance of such punishment). In these forays Klansmen demolished brothels and whipped suspected prostitutes, adulterers, and wife beaters. On occasion a Klan leader might use this penchant for social regulation to recruit members: a North Carolina legislator and Klan leader promised that members would be able to "protect [their] families from the darkies." But Klan leaders more often denounced unauthorized regulators, insisting they were driving away farm hands and risking federal reprisals. Like army commanders, leading Klansmen thus deplored some of their followers' excesses, but unlike army officers Klan leaders had no punishments to enforce their disapproval. Indeed, the Klan's political successes were likely assisted by common whites' freelance terrorism. Poorer folk may have been willing to sustain the Klan because they were also free to use it for their own ends, in contrast to the army's insistence on restricting soldiers' activities.

Federal prosecutions under the Enforcement Acts may have shut down the Klan in the early 1870s, but conservative whites' determination to overthrow Republican state governments remained unshaken. Some of the governments had already fallen: internal Republican divisions had enabled conservative Democrats to regain power in upper South states such as Tennessee, and Klan violence and intimidation of black voters contributed to a Democratic victory in Alabama. Republicans clung to power in several Southern states in the mid-1870s, but conservatives were determined to complete their takeover of the South.

Veterans had fully shaken off their postwar lethargy and were leading the way in reasserting white supremacy. Indeed, apathy about Reconstruction had shifted to the North, where politicians who had once been champions of civil rights for freedpeople were now preoccupied with an economic depression that began in 1873 and with scandals in the administration of President Ulysses S. Grant.

A case in point from Mississippi will illustrate the extent to which Confederate veterans had become reinvigorated. Mississippi's black majority sustained state and local Republican governments until 1875. Then, conservative whites, taking heart from dramatic nationwide gains by the Democrats in the previous year's congressional elections, intensified their campaign to oust the Republicans. To carry out their plan, conservatives would have to mobilize the white vote and ruthlessly intimidate black voters. White mobilization had already begun before 1875 with the formation of local "taxpayers' leagues," groups that called for lower taxes and less public spending while insisting that Republican governments were rife with corruption.

By the summer of 1875 the protests had developed into a political movement, with the coming legislative elections the target. Democratic clubs sprang up around the state, and Confederate veterans were in the forefront of their resurgence. The newspaper in Crystal Springs in south-central Mississippi, for example, published a list of Democratic club members, who comprised nearly three-fourths of the town's taxpayers. Where Confederate veterans had been reluctant even to vote ten years earlier, they were now eager to join the movement to recapture the legislature. Former Confederate soldiers were more than twice as likely as noncombatants to join the Democratic club in Crystal Springs.

Once organized, Confederate veterans and their fellow Democrats gave the 1875 election the air of a military operation. Democratic clubs held parades that featured color guards, cannon, double-file marching, and the "rebel yell." Blacks in Vicksburg complained that white men were "going around the streets at night in soldiers clothes and making the colored people run for their lives." Conservative whites had indeed declared war on African-American and white Republicans. Determined, in the words of a newspaper editor, to "carry the election peaceably if we can, forcibly if we must," heavily armed bands of whites disrupted Republican rallies, assassinated Republican politicians, and warned black men not to vote, no longer bothering with the disguises of Ku Klux Klan days.

On election day Democrats prevented the distribution of Republican ballots, harassed those blacks who did come out to

vote, and tampered with the ballot boxes. The result, not surprisingly, was a sweeping Democratic victory and a commanding majority in the Mississippi legislature. Also not
surprisingly, Democrats valued wartime leadership in putting
men into office. In the Mississippi legislative elections of 1877
(whose records are more complete than those of 1875), Confederate leadership was even more important than it had been
a decade earlier. In races contested between veterans and noncombatants, once again Confederate service made little difference by itself, but having been an officer quadrupled a
candidate's chances of being elected. Indeed, high Confederate
rank became so associated with elective office that the remainder of the century has been identified as the "rule of the
brigadiers" across the South.

In 1877, as part of a deal that sorted out the disputed results
of the previous year's presidential election, federal troops were
withdrawn from Louisiana and South Carolina, and the last
Republican governments in the South fell to the Democrats.
Southerners thereby completed a remarkable turnabout—the
same people who had been unable to mount a large-scale resistance during the war were ultimately successful in doing so afterward.

Despite their dominant role in this resistance, Confederate
veterans in the 1870s were affected by the same public amnesia
about the war itself that was found in the North. Veterans' return to militarism in their campaign to topple Republican
governments, and politicians' campaign references to their
wartime service, were not part of any mass movement to relive the war. There were, to be sure, some Confederate organizations in the 1870s: the Association of the Army of Northern
Virginia and the Southern Historical Society, the most influ-
ential of such groups, devoted themselves to enshrining Confederate heroes and differentiating the South's cause from its

defeat. But these were organizations of the Confederate leadership, not the rank and file; only a few thousand Southerners joined during the 1870s. Most veterans preferred to commemorate their fallen comrades in local ceremonies rather than to celebrate the abilities of Virginia generals or contemplate the course of the war.

But just as Union veterans experienced a renewal of group consciousness in the 1880s, so did former Confederate soldiers. The immediate cause of the renewal was different in the South—there was no massive pension crusade to unify Confederate veterans. While the federal government pondered ways to spend its surplus, the Democratic state governments of the South cut back sharply on social spending; aside from a few tax exemptions for veterans, there was little public assistance available to ex-Confederate soldiers.

Instead, the changes in American society that worried Union veterans and helped to cause a public nostalgia for the Civil War also distressed Southerners. People in the South knew about the explosive growth of cities, the enormous increase in foreign immigration, and the expansion of industrial corporations; they realized that the nation's heroes were no longer presidents or military men but corporate lords, such as oil magnate John D. Rockefeller, financier J. Pierpont Morgan, and steel baron Andrew Carnegie, none of whom had fought in the Civil War; and Southerners watched the relationship between owners and workers grow into violent confrontations between increasingly assertive workers and intransigent employers. These developments were concentrated in the North, but the South felt their effects: it had its own vigorous debate about the merits of economic development, and Southern companies had their share of labor disputes. Southerners feared that worse was yet to come as Northern trends penetrated their communities. And in spite of their recapture of state governments, many whites believed that blacks still posed a threat to their control of Southern society.

Americans who were perplexed by these changes tried a number of means to overcome their insecurities. Fraternal orders like the Masons and Odd Fellows, which flourished in the late nineteenth century, fostered common bonds and offered a refuge from the outside world. Putting a stop to disturbing trends was another promising strategy. Rural political movements tried to reverse the concentration of power in the hands of industrialists and financiers. But turning back the clock became especially popular. The Civil War now seemed a time of selflessness and heroism compared to the grasping meanness of the century's closing decades.

Southerners had their own version of these efforts, and Confederate veterans often took the lead. The Patrons of Husbandry, popularly known as the Grange, flourished in the Midwest and South in the 1870s. Begun as fraternal and educational gatherings, Grange meetings brought together farmers who complained about exploitation by railroads, banks, and merchants. Grangers experimented with cooperatives to pool their buying and selling power, and they pushed for state laws to regulate the rates they paid to warehouses and railroads. In the South, Granges were often dominated by Confederate veterans who sought to revive the traditional privilege of white landowners. Two-thirds of the charter members of one central Mississippi Grange branch were Confederate veterans, and a speaker at another branch insisted on "less freedom and more protection to property." The Southern Grange thus became part of the drive to restore white supremacy.

Financial problems with cooperatives and vigorous opposition by businessmen sent the Grange into decline in the late

1870s, and its cause was taken up by the Farmers' Alliance in the 1880s. The Alliance was more openly political than the Grange had been—it put up its own candidates for state offices and Congress, and lobbied for federal aid in marketing crops—and was especially strong in the South. Again Confederates, most of whom were farmers, flocked to the cause, and they put their stamp on the movement. A Georgia Alliance leader and Confederate veteran warned that "we are fighting now against a foe more insidious [than the Union]," and the Tennessee Alliance described its members as "an army of veterans who are so nobly and determinedly resisting the efforts of combined capital."

Encouraged by their electoral success—in 1890 six Alliance-backed candidates won governors' races, three were elected to the U.S. Senate, and fifty won seats in the U.S. House—but frustrated by inaction on legislation to help farmers, agrarian activists formed a national political party. The Populists, as the new party's adherents called themselves, set their sights on the 1892 presidential election and reached out to other workers by endorsing such measures as an eight-hour day for industry.

The Populists also created a dilemma for Southerners. Democrats, now firmly in control of Southern politics, had tolerated and sometimes joined the Farmers' Alliance, but agrarian activists intent on becoming a competing party were a serious threat. Democrats relentlessly denounced the new party, insinuating that Populists were actively seeking African Americans' support and would eventually subvert white supremacy. Democrats pleaded for white solidarity in defeating the alleged biracial menace, and their pleas inevitably included an appeal to old soldiers' loyalty.

But loyalties were not so simple for veterans. Many Populist leaders, moving over from the Farmers' Alliance, were themselves Confederate veterans. Nor were veterans willing to abandon the agrarian cause so quickly; moreover, a few Southern states had already restricted blacks' right to vote, thereby easing racist fears of populism. An estimate of voting behavior in Mississippi reveals veterans' divided loyalties as well as their interest in politics. Fewer than one in five nonveterans voted in the 1892 election, and hardly any voted for the Populists; half of all Confederate veterans turned out for the election, however, and about half of those who voted chose Populist candidates (James B. Weaver, the Populist presidential nominee, received about 9 percent of the vote nationwide).

Populism rapidly declined after the 1896 election, but veterans, now mostly in their fifties, had shown they were still in the vanguard of political activism, just as they had been in their twenties when they went to war for another political cause. And some of them had also shown they were willing to reject the party they had helped to revive after the war.

Veterans also participated eagerly in the effort to turn back the clock. In the 1880s Confederate veterans formed groups that were meant to have a broader appeal than did the elite Association of the Army of Northern Virginia and similar organizations. The new groups grew rapidly, and in 1889 they created a new national order, the United Confederate Veterans. Membership figures for the UCV are imprecise, but Gaines Foster has estimated that from one-fourth to one-third of Confederate veterans joined the organization in the 1890s, roughly the same as the proportion of Union veterans in the Grand Army of the Republic at its height. Like the GAR, the UCV was led by local businessmen, but significant numbers of farmers, artisans, and unskilled workers also joined. With this broadening of membership came a broadening of purposes for Confederate veterans.

Confederate monuments, which were originally memorials

to the dead, now became shrines to the common soldier. The UCV and its women's auxiliary, the United Daughters of the Confederacy, took an active role in local monument-building, and they deemphasized funereal designs. New monuments were now as likely to be in a town square as in a cemetery, and most monuments displayed a generic foot soldier rather than a symbol of grief. Instead of mourning the dead soldiers and their cause as did the early monuments, the new memorials admonished the public to honor living as well as deceased veterans and to imitate their example of loyalty and self-sacrifice.

The centerpiece of the UCV's broadened appeal was the reunion. Veterans had often held local barbecues and state meetings, but by the 1890s the annual UCV reunion overshadowed all local gatherings. Tens of thousands of former Confederates poured into cities such as Birmingham and Richmond, where they relived the war and recaptured old values. As they had in the army, veterans at a reunion could feel both local identity and membership in a larger movement, and they could reaffirm their willingness to fight for southern womanhood and social stability. UCV camps selected young women to participate in the reunions, honoring them as representatives of women's devotion to the Confederacy (even though the UCV's view of women's role was as sharply limited as the GAR's; the organization vehemently objected to a UDC plan to build a monument depicting an assertive woman, for example). UCV members also relished their role as defenders of social order. Referring to violence between owners and workers in the 1890s, the UCV's commander boasted that he could raise "an army of old soldiers" to put down the troubles, "every man of whom [would] fight to the death to preserve the Union and command respect for the old flag."

At the same time the UCV backed away from some of the combative pro-Southern rhetoric of earlier Confederate groups. These Southern partisans had insisted that secession be viewed solely as a principled act of self-rule and that the Confederacy's defeat be seen purely as the inevitable result of the North's superior numbers. The UCV, for its part, did press for the Southern viewpoint in textbooks and argued for the "War Between the States" as the proper name for the conflict, but the new generation of veterans' leaders was less strident in vindicating the Confederacy than earlier spokesmen had been. Instead the new leaders were more open to reconciliation with their former enemies. Blue-Gray reunions flourished from the 1880s onward, as Union and Confederate veterans got together on battlefields and at Memorial Day celebrations. Although many Southerners remained opposed to reconciliation, the trend continued, aided by the Spanish-American War in 1898, which allowed partisans on both sides to support a common cause.

This upsurge in veterans' activity was accompanied by increased public concern for ex-Confederate soldiers and their survivors. The Democrats' cutbacks in their states' social spending had left little public assistance for veterans until the 1880s. Then, as public interest in the war revived, so did public alarm about reports of veterans in poorhouses and stories of impoverished widows and children. Prodded by veterans' advocates who pointed to such reports and to increasingly generous pensions for Union veterans, Southern state legislators considered providing their own aid to former Confederate soldiers.

State aid had its opponents, including veterans who insisted that public assistance would undermine ex-soldiers' manly self-reliance, but by the early 1890s most of the former Confederate states had resumed their assistance to veterans. One form of aid was the pension: states provided a scale of payments to disabled and destitute veterans and their survivors.

Nine states were paying Confederate pensions by the early 1890s, but their limited willingness and resources for social spending kept pensions modest. Fewer than 10 percent of Confederate veterans and widows received pensions in the early 1890s, and the average payment was $40 a year at a time when more than two-thirds of Union veterans were receiving an average of $160 a year. Later in the decade, Louisiana and Texas became the last ex-Confederate states to enact veterans' pensions.

At about the same time Southern legislators were acting on pensions, they also debated establishing veterans' homes. Again there was opposition—from Alliancemen and Populists in Georgia, who saw soldiers' home advocates as elite urbanites, and from wartime Unionists in East Tennessee—but by 1901 seven former Confederate states had opened homes. Substantial numbers of Confederate veterans came to these homes by the early years of the new century.

The characteristics of those who came to soldiers' homes illustrate the harshness of life for some in the postwar South. In a sample of Tennessee soldiers' home residents, only one-third had suffered a war wound, but 90 percent had previously received some form of public aid (usually food, clothing, or other assistance furnished by county officials). One-third of the men were single, and two-thirds had no family members to help them; 20 percent had been in a poorhouse, and another 20 percent had been unemployed for five years or longer.

Inside the homes, residents found a devotion to discipline similar to that of the Union veterans' homes. Like the Northern homes, Southern institutions boasted of their superiority to poorhouses—soldiers' homes had attractive locations and prided themselves on their generosity to residents—but their officials were also ambivalent about the residents' character. Those who sought shelter in the homes were, after all, heroes of the Southern cause, but administrators were nonetheless suspicious of individuals who could not support themselves. As a result, administrators imposed military rules and work requirements on residents, not only to keep the homes operating smoothly but also, in the words of a Georgia official, to "reform and improve [residents'] behavior and deportment."

Life in Southern homes was punctuated by contests of will between administrators and residents who were convinced that officials were autocratic killjoys. As in the Northern homes, and as in the Civil War armies, the struggles were sometimes furtive, as residents defied rules against drinking, theft, and unauthorized leave, and were at other times open and violent: the Georgia home witnessed a fistfight between the superintendent and a resident, and a resident attacked the superintendent of the Texas home with a cane.

Confederate veterans at the other end of the social scale had a different problem as the nineteenth century neared its end. Ex-soldiers, especially those who had been officers, were used to being at the center of the white community and were accustomed to dominating state and local politics. By the late 1880s, however, they could see their uniquely privileged position slipping away. As old age approached and the postwar generation began to reach maturity, veterans began to worry about their legacy. A South Carolinian wrote that "most of the young men are willing to turn their backs on everything that we were taught to regard as sacred." Building monuments and keeping an eye on textbooks helped, but conventional ways of conveying the war's importance were not always satisfying. "You children simply don't understand," the father of Georgian Mell Barrett would say in frustration when war stories failed to impress his listeners.

Another kind of legacy was more appealing to some veterans. In the years after "Redemption," as Democrats called

their takeover of Southern governments in the 1870s, race relations had remained unsettled. Southern whites quickly established barriers of segregation anywhere the sexes as well as
the races might mix—in hotels, restaurants, parks, and railroad cars. Yet in places where men and women were not likely
to meet, such as country stores, cotton gins, and saloons, there
were few efforts to separate the races. And black men continued to vote in large numbers, even though their actual political influence was minuscule. Redeemer politicians tolerated
black voting and a few Republican candidates, as long as
whites could control the outcome of elections and manipulate
black officeholders. If they felt threatened by black assertive-
ness, whites would resort to the familiar methods of fraud, intimidation of voters, and violence. A Mississippian admitted
in 1890, for example, that "there has not been a full vote and a
fair count in Mississippi since 1875," and a Louisiana observer
noted that "after the polls are closed the election really be-
gins."

Many white Southerners were satisfied with these arrangements. A few states tried legal restrictions on blacks' voting,
such as poll taxes and cumbersome voting procedures, but further efforts to control voting usually met with firm resistance.
"Why agitate and convulse the country when quiet is so desir-
able and important for the public welfare?" asked Mississippi's governor in 1888, and Louisianians were unwilling to
upset "the existing order of things, with which the people are
satisfied," by toughening voting regulations.

But in Mississippi, which would lead the way in permanently disfranchising African Americans, such reluctance
gave way to a wave of white insecurity by 1890. Republicans
now controlled the White House and Congress, raising fears
of new federal voting-rights laws; whites were worried that
the 1890 census would show a widening black majority in

Mississippi; and, according to historian David Donald, the Confederate generation's fear for its legacy was becoming overwhelming. A former colonel underscored his generation's anxiety about the way it controlled politics: "The old men of the present generation can't afford to die and leave their children with shot guns in their hands, a lie on their mouths and perjury on their souls, in order to defeat the negroes." These men had taken up arms for white supremacy once in the 1860s and again in the mid-1870s, and the time for permanently securing their prize was slipping away. A new governor removed the last obstacle to a constitutional convention, and an election of delegates was ordered for July 1890.

Historians have noted that only 15 percent of Mississippi's eligible voters turned out for the delegate elections and have pointed out that this first "disfranchising convention" was sharply split between the cotton belt and the upcountry, but Confederate veterans were also important in the campaign to change Mississippi's constitution. Estimates of voting behavior suggest deep differences in voter turnout. Very few black men were willing or allowed to vote in an election that would probably lead to their disfranchisement (but those who did vote helped to elect the convention's only Republican). Not many whites voted either: only about one-third bothered to vote for convention delegates. But Confederate veterans, who were 22 percent of the white electorate, were serious about rewriting the constitution—an estimated two-thirds of veterans turned out to vote for convention delegates.

Veterans were equally serious about designing the voting restrictions. Fewer than 40 percent of the Mississippi convention's delegates were ex-Confederate soldiers, but the franchise committee was their preserve. Nearly three-quarters of the committee's members were veterans; committee members were older men and were disproportionately from the cotton belt, but being an ex-soldier was far more likely than age or locale to get a delegate selected to this all-important committee.

The delegates met from August 12 through the end of October and produced a new constitution that was intended to bar most African Americans from voting. A prospective voter would have to negotiate a maze of residency requirements, poll taxes, literacy tests, and other obstacles aimed at disqualifying blacks. These restrictions did eliminate almost all the black vote (and some of the white vote as well), and they impressed political leaders elsewhere.

Indeed, South Carolina followed Mississippi's lead four years later, with similar support from veterans. In the referendum that authorized a constitutional convention, fewer than half of white men voted. An estimated 80 percent of Confederate veterans voted, however, and they favored the convention by two to one. But before other states held constitutional conventions, the struggle between Populists and Democrats had divided veterans' loyalties. Many Populist leaders were unwilling to disqualify poor whites or blacks who were potential supporters, and they denounced proposals for disfranchisement. When Alabama held a referendum in 1901, veterans' loyalties were split between the proconvention Democratic position and the opposition advocated by Populists. Veterans' role was also limited when these later conventions met. Only one-fourth of delegates were Confederate veterans in the conventions held in Alabama and Louisiana, and veterans were less dominant on franchise committees than they had been in Mississippi. All the ex-Confederate states eventually adopted some form of voting restrictions, but by the turn of the century a new generation of political leaders had emerged, one more concerned with taxes and business regulation than with preserving the spirit of Redemption.

The movement to disfranchise black men was nonetheless a remarkable example of public deference to an activist minority. In no Southern state was constitutional disfranchisement a mass movement; voter turnout in convention-related elections duplicated the low participation in Mississippi and South Carolina. But, as in these two states, apparent apathy could mask real interest—Confederate veterans could come out in strength for convention elections, and veterans could dominate the key committee at a convention. It was determination, not sheer numbers, that ensured white supremacy in Southern states, and that determination indicated a generation convinced of its special authority.

This special authority was as evident among constitution-writers as it was among veterans' activists. Although the UCV said little in public about disfranchisement, its leaders sounded remarkably like advocates. The UCV constitution endorsed, for example, a campaign "to instill into our descendants proper veneration for the spirit and glory of their fathers," while the Confederate veteran who headed the Mississippi convention declared that the delegates' goal was "to preserve the morals of this and the coming generation." Other men eventually took over the effort to enshrine white supremacy, but veterans' role in beginning the movement was in itself a notable feat.

Approximately 350,000 Confederate veterans lived to see the end of the nineteenth century. Most of them had remained aloof from the growth of cities, towns, and industry that was changing the South. Younger Southerners had already begun to turn away from farming: at the turn of the century, just over half of Southern whites in their thirties were farmers. Confederate veterans, however, older men who had come primarily from farming areas, resisted change, and nearly two-thirds remained farmers as the century ended. It is common for the elderly to oppose change and relive the past, but it was not just age that impelled veterans to their extraordinary efforts to reverse the clock. In UCV parades and at Memorial Day celebrations, ex-soldiers reminded everyone they were guardians not simply of the past but of an unparalleled experience that remained alive as a warning against tampering with social stability. By initiating the effort to restrict the vote, some veterans went even farther in exercising their special authority: they attempted to prevent future generations from changing a key feature of the social order.

Confederate veterans had fewer tangible signs of special status than did Union veterans—their pensions were a fraction of Union veterans' payments, and a much smaller proportion of ex-Confederates wound up in soldiers' homes—but ex-Confederates had nonetheless made an unmistakable mark on their society.

7

Civil War Veterans in the Twentieth Century

IN THE SPRING of 1910 federal census takers went from door to door to collect information for the thirteenth census of the United States. For only the second time (and the first time that can help modern historians, because detailed information from the 1890 census was destroyed in a fire), the enumerators asked older men if they had served in the Civil War.

By 1910 fewer than one-third of the war's original Union survivors were still alive. Mostly in their late sixties and early seventies, the remaining veterans were a reminder of a different America. Eighty percent were native-born whites, compared with fewer than 60 percent of elderly Northern civilians. According to the author Bruce Catton, who grew up in a Michigan town in the early twentieth century, Civil War veterans were "men set apart" in other ways as well. Catton saw veterans as "the keepers of [their community's] patriotic traditions," because "years ago they had marched thousands of miles to legendary battlefields."

For veterans who wished to sustain this aura of uniqueness, the Grand Army of the Republic remained active in the new century, holding its encampments for comradeship and continuing its work of "patriotic instruction." The GAR was the ideal organization for veterans like the father of the writer Sherwood Anderson. According to his son, Irwin Anderson learned in the years following the war "that he would never be a hero again, that all the rest of his life he would have to build on those days."

Nevertheless, a large number of Union veterans, probably a majority, never joined the GAR. We might assume they considered themselves citizens first and soldiers second, and were willing to consign their wartime experiences to the past. But few of them completely forgot their service. By 1900 the Pension Bureau had made old age (defined as sixty-five) a "disability" for pension purposes; in 1904 the Bureau changed the definition to sixty-two and in 1907 Congress made the ruling into law. Since almost all Union veterans were now older than sixty-two, these changes finally made Civil War "service" pensions a reality.

As a result, previously ineligible ex-soldiers reminded the Pension Bureau of their service and asked for a pension. By 1910 virtually all living Union veterans were on the pension rolls. The average payment was $172 a year, though high rank or multiple disabilities could qualify a former soldier for as much as $1,200 per year. As sociologist Theda Skocpol has pointed out, this was a far more generous pension system than those in Europe at the time, although European pensions were meant for much broader classes of the elderly.

Veterans' pensions were also a higher proportion of typical yearly wages than were the Social Security payments that would begin in the 1930s. Did veterans' pensions serve as an early form of retirement program? Retirement had a different meaning in the early twentieth century than it does today. Some medical experts and business leaders were urging, in the name of efficiency, that employers replace older workers with younger ones, but there was no widely accepted stopping point for a man's working life. Instead, most men expected to withdraw from employment gradually, phasing out physical chores while remaining active as givers of advice. Three-fourths of American men aged sixty to seventy-five reported in 1910 that they still had an occupation.

But the proportion of men who had quit working had risen since 1900, and these nonemployed men were especially likely to be Union veterans. Even when we control for age and material wealth such as ownership of a home, we find that veterans were less likely than nonveterans to be working (this finding applies to white men, since there are few African-American veterans in the census sample). This difference in employment was not simply due to veterans' health problems stemming from the war. In 1890, when fewer than one-third of veterans received pensions, they had been *more* likely to be working than were nonveterans of the same age. Since almost all Union veterans were drawing a pension in 1910, it is likely that a regular income from the federal treasury (plus, in many states, additional state and local veterans' pensions) allowed men to stop working earlier than they would have otherwise.

Veterans' pensions, like the early Social Security payments, were not meant to be a pensioner's sole source of support: an advocate of the 1907 expansion of pensions expected them to be only "a small pittance," enough to keep veterans from "being compelled to go hungry the balance of their few years." Yet the pensions made a difference, allowing a substantial number of veterans to be pioneers in retiring from work, just as the first Social Security payments helped to spur a much larger exodus of older workers from the labor force in the 1930s.

It was widely believed that Civil War pensions also influenced the behavior of women. Attitudes toward women that we have seen throughout this book have followed a pattern. Most Northerners in the nineteenth century revered women who conformed to their assigned roles—care-giver, preserver of home and family, admiring companion—but distrusted women who did not conform—prostitutes, extreme Confederate partisans, and, later, women who would exploit Union veterans and the federal government's generosity. A few pension advocates lavished praise on widows whom they considered virtuous, that is, those who did all they could "to teach lessons of patriotism and pure love of country to their children." At the same time social critics were warning that "there has grown up in the United States a race of widows that is increasing in numbers and degenerating in worth." It was believed that these widows lived with men without marrying, to keep their widow's pension. As a result, conditions that included an income test were eventually added to widows' application requirements, and members of Congress and Pension Bureau officials advocated inquiring into female applicants' character before their pensions were approved.

Social critics and government officials were even more alarmed about another class of women. A pension official insisted that "there is a great abuse of the pension laws by young women, who marry old soldiers for no other reason than to live on the pension money after their husbands are gone." To guard against these "designing women," as they were called, Congress took such steps as disqualifying widows from pensions under the Dependent Pension Act if they had married a veteran after 1890, but there is little evidence that officials' fears were justified.

If "pension marriages" were indeed common, the 1910 census should show a clear difference between veterans' and nonveterans' marital status. Commentators argued that designing women had continued to prey on veterans even after the Dependent Pension Act; if critics were correct, there should have been considerably more married veterans than married civilians in 1910, and veterans' wives should have been younger than wives of civilians. But there are no striking differences: veterans were slightly more likely to be married than were elderly civilians, but veterans' wives tended to be slightly *older* than civilians' wives. Some women undoubtedly did marry elderly veterans for their pensions, but they were the exception and not the rule.

Although the population of Union veterans was dwindling in 1910, soldiers' homes were still growing. The federal homes admitted more than 3,700 new residents in 1900 and maintained a total population of 19,000; by 1910 the population of the homes had reached 20,000, and an additional 12,000 Union veterans were living in state-operated soldiers' homes. The nature of the homes and the ex-soldiers they housed had changed since the early postwar decades. In the early years most residents had been foreign-born and single (foreign-born men were more likely to be single than were the native-born), and the majority sought care because of a war wound. By the turn of the century, fewer wives and families were able to care for disabled and impoverished ex-soldiers, and married or widowed native-born veterans came to dominate the homes' population. Now men with diseases (which included, according to official definitions, old age) outnumbered those with wounds. The homes had become old-age refuges: residents, increasingly unable to handle the homes' maintenance, had to be replaced by hired staff, and medical personnel and facilities had to be steadily expanded to deal with the health problems of aging veterans.

But if soldiers' home residents had changed, official ambivalence about them had not. Public officials were so pleased with the spacious grounds and imposing buildings they had provided that they believed the homes could improve public character. Enthusiasts described soldiers' homes as parklike havens of rest and reflection for visitors; the homes would "keep the fire of patriotism burning, that the people may not forget the men who stood by the nation in its hour of peril." Yet the authorities were not as pleased with the men themselves. According to officials of the Ohio federal home, the residents had become more insubordinate with age: "There is less self-restraint among them than among younger men; consequently some of them need constant watching and firm handling."

As usual among authorities concerned with self-control, drinking was the offense that most worried the homes' managers. As it had been when they were soldiers, drinking continued to be among residents' favorite pastimes; their indulgence ranged from an occasional spree in a nearby town to alcoholics' compulsive drinking of smuggled-in liquor. Soldiers' home personnel were among the earliest adherents of the view that alcoholism was a disease, but a remedy was elusive. Seeking in the 1890s to cure alcoholics, officials brought in purveyors of popular remedies, among them Dr. Leslie Keeley's "gold cure," a type of aversion therapy. Seeking to supervise consumption among other drinkers, officials opened beer halls at the federal homes around the turn of the century. The halls appeared to satisfy managers and residents alike and even won the approval of most of the homes' chaplains, but temperance activists were infuriated by the spectacle of government officials selling liquor to former soldiers. Insisting that self-control be maintained even among disabled men in their sixties and seventies, one antiliquor member of Congress demanded that the houses take away residents' alcohol and instead "help them to build up the wasted manhood of their earlier years and live the evening of life temperate, sober, upright, worthy citizens." Congress bowed to this pressure and ordered the beer halls closed in 1907. Residents returned to drinking off the premises and smuggling liquor into the homes, and alcohol-related offenses increased sharply at several homes.

Elderly Union veterans were thus both a privileged and a burdened population. They did have opportunities that were unavailable to their civilian peers. In the new century nearly all ex-Union soldiers could claim a generous pension and many were able to retire, provided they could ignore the condemnation of some social critics. The *New York Times* believed that most ablebodied pensioners were "bummers, deserters, [and] sturdy beggars," and the editors of the magazine *The Nation* declared that "men who would die rather than enter a poorhouse and live at the cost of the community, see no wrong in living at the cost of the taxpayer, believing that, because they donned a uniform forty-nine years ago, they now have an inherent right to aid in their old age."

Former Union soldiers who were impoverished still had an alternative to the poorhouse, but they continued to differ with soldiers' home managers over the nature of a veteran's obligations. Managers saw self-discipline as the least they could expect from residents in exchange for the government's generosity, but many residents saw withholding of their pensions as high-handed, and the policy on drinking, one of an old soldier's few pleasures, as inconsistent. But the homes also offered security and comfort, and as their health grew worse and their options dwindled, veterans continued to seek admission to the homes; only after 1910 did the homes' population begin a continuous decline.

By 1920 fewer than 15 percent of the Civil War's original survivors were still alive, and World War I had added more than 4 million new veterans to occupy the government's attention. The Pension Bureau and the national soldiers' homes were merged into the new Veterans Administration in 1930, and the few survivors of the generation that had preserved the Union and once dominated national politics were now relics of a bygone age.

The Spanish-American War of 1898 was a turning point for many Confederate veterans, and it set the tone for their activities in the twentieth century. The Grand Army of the Republic supported the war, but fighting a foreign enemy was more than simply wise policy to ex-Confederates—this was a chance to prove that Confederate veterans were patriots, not rebels, and to remove the remaining stigma of defeat. Some Confederate veterans were young enough to serve in the war and drew high praise from Southerners, but ex-soldiers' influence extended much further. Young soldiers in the Spanish-American War were fond of using the rebel yell, and a Confederate veteran's son wrote that he and his fellows "owe you of '61 a debt of untold gratitude and admiration for the noble examples & high ideals set for us to follow."

The Spanish-American War's aftermath underscored Confederate veterans' worries about the future. Fighting in Spain's former colonies did not end with the formal armistice of August 1898. Filipino resistance forces fought American control as they had fought the Spanish, and it was not until 1902 that American troops, gunning down women and children and burning villages in response to the rebels' guerrilla warfare, managed to subdue native resistance in the Philippines. American soldiers from the South expressed little sympathy with the Filipinos' desire for self-rule. A few leading Southerners appreciated the parallels between the Filipinos' struggle and the Confederacy's, and a senator from Arkansas refused "to force upon an unwilling people principles and policies against which Lee fought," but many more Southerners insisted that order and stability were the key American interests in the Philippines. The *Atlanta Constitution* demanded that American troops "vindicate the authority of our flag," a senator from the same state insisted that the United States establish a government "capable of maintaining law and order," and a young soldier from Tennessee even wanted to "carry on a war as Sherman did on his march to the sea." The primary lesson of the Civil War that came down to Southerners at the turn of the century was the primacy of order, whether in government, labor relations, or relations between the races.

Former Confederates felt vindicated by the Spanish-American War. Participation in the war "healed many scars," wrote a Southerner, and another believed that "the whole South is to be recognized and rehabilitated." Leading veterans in the North and the South became increasingly conciliatory: in the first decade of the new century the federal government assumed responsibility for Confederate graves in the North and finally returned captured Confederate flags, actions applauded by most Confederate veterans, and in the next decade more than fifty thousand veterans from both sides attended the fiftieth anniversary of the Battle of Gettysburg.

At the same time annual gatherings were losing their focus as public reenactments of the Confederate army experience. As we have seen, United Confederate Veterans' reunions in the 1890s were meant to impress on the public the comradeship and patriotism of Confederate soldiers. After 1900, however, reunions were increasingly dominated by social functions for the elite (one ex-soldier decided that "Reunions of the Confederate veterans as latterly conducted are not for [the rank and file]"), and were increasingly given over to commercial advertising. Whether it was their advancing age, their dwindling numbers, or a combination of causes, veterans in the new century were becoming less jealous of the Confederate tradition they had worked to publicize and pass on to the next generation.

As ex-Confederates grew older they also relied more on pensions. Some states expanded eligibility for pensions (though they still required applicants to affirm their poverty), and more elderly veterans made use of the payments. By 1910 approximately one-fourth of Confederate veterans were drawing a state pension, and the payments, small as they were, appear to have encouraged some to retire. Average pensions in 1910 were still less than $50 per year, but 30 percent of Confederate veterans had stopped working, compared with fewer than 20 percent of elderly Southern noncombatants.

In the next decade most Southern states raised their pension amounts, and Kentucky, Missouri, and Oklahoma began paying pensions. By 1920 the average payment had passed $100, and about half of all Confederate veterans were on the pension rolls. But half had not applied at a time when virtually every Union veteran was drawing a federal pension. Confederate veterans were still more than twice as likely to be living on farms as were ex-Union soldiers; suspicion of government programs ran high in the countryside, and any declaration of poverty stained not only the individual but his kinfolk as well.

The rural aversion to government aid was also evident among veterans who went to Confederate soldiers' homes. The population of soldiers' homes across the South reached its peak at about 2,400 during the decade after 1910. This was less than 10 percent of the population of federal and state homes for Union soldiers, and in a sample of residents just over 40 percent had been farmers, compared with nearly two-thirds of all ex-Confederates.

But if rural Southerners were more reluctant to seek shelter in these homes, the homes themselves followed much the same course as did their Union counterparts. By the decade after 1910, residents were typically in their mid-seventies, and health care for the elderly had become a main goal of the homes. Although the Southern homes were small (six of the fifteen homes had fewer than one hundred residents in 1915, while a typical federal home had more than one thousand), most of them now had their own hospital, with staff physicians, nurses, and modern equipment. Officials boasted of a death rate lower than outside the homes, and there is evidence for their claim: men who passed their seventieth birthday in the Missouri home, for example, could expect to live for thirteen years, compared with nine years among the general population in states that kept uniform death records.

State legislatures were willing to pay for this expensive care, demonstrating the considerable hold Confederate veterans still maintained over their descendants. Louisiana's appropriation to operate its home jumped from $40,000 in 1914 to $65,000 in 1920, for example, and North Carolina's went from $35,000 to $60,000; in Georgia, care for veterans (pensions and the soldiers' home) took up more than 20 percent of the budget in the early twentieth century.

In spite of physical changes in the homes, the climate of discipline and resistance remained. As in Union homes, Southern officials expected elderly residents to be docile, but they were not. In the decade after 1910, officials at the Louisiana home charged a number of residents, most of whom were in their seventies, with a variety of offenses, including drunkenness, fighting, and climbing the institution's fence. Defiance of the rules continued after 1920: the Georgia home expelled a resident for selling liquor in 1926, and the Missouri home dismissed an eighty-year-old resident for insubordination in 1925 and an eighty-six-year-old for fighting in 1932. Most Confederate homes eventually admitted women residents—wives, widows, and occasionally daughters and nieces of veterans—

but the institutions remained predominantly male, with characteristic male contention over the limits of authority and obedience.

Yet the old Confederates were dying off, and most of the homes closed in the 1930s and 1940s. Ex-Confederates' numbers were shrinking everywhere: of approximately 100,000 ex-Confederates in 1920, only about 35,000 were alive in 1930, and perhaps a thousand lived to see the nation's second-costliest war begin in 1941. The ranks of their old adversaries were likewise thinning. There were fewer than 300,000 ex-Union soldiers in 1920, under 100,000 in 1930, and only a few thousand survived in 1940.

The last known Union soldier was Louis Nicholas, who had been a drummer with the Sixth Missouri regiment and who died in 1957. The last known former Confederate soldier was Walter Williams, a forage-master who had served with the Fifth Virginia and who died in 1959. But the last man who had seen some form of Civil War service had, perhaps fittingly, served both sides. Sylvester Magee, born a slave in Covington County, Mississippi, was at first a servant in the Confederate army but ran away to the Union forces, who assigned him to burial details at Vicksburg. Magee died not far from his original home on October 15, 1971.

8

The Civil War Experience in Perspective

WHAT WAS THE meaning of being a Civil War veteran, and how did that meaning differ between Union and Confederate veterans? We have seen marked differences in background and character among the men who joined the two armies. Both sides drew broadly from their populations, but laborers—skilled and unskilled—were especially likely to fight for the Union, and wealthier, slaveholding Southerners were especially likely to join the Confederate army. And while Union soldiers worried about restraining their sentiments and impulses, Confederates tended to express their emotions freely and to lash out at affronts to their honor from friend or foe. There is little in soldiers' writings to indicate that the war fundamentally changed these traits, and traces of them remained long after the war. The GAR's extraordinary concern with self-control and the exceptional fierceness of confrontations in Southern soldiers' homes suggest the depth of character differences between the sections.

Yet warfare is in other ways an equalizer, and we have seen evidence of that as well. A call to arms seeks out and finds common sentiments, even among populations with different motivations for fighting. Mobilizing a popular army exploits loyalty to the community, the desire to conform with peers, the need to keep faith with tradition, and the urge to prove one's masculinity. As a result, young men on both sides led the rush to sign up, and they boasted of their ability to make short work of the other side; in more reflective moments most of them worried about home and community, and soldiers on both sides claimed kinship with the patriots of the American Revolution. Enlisted men on both sides discovered how much they disliked taking orders from men they considered no better than themselves, a dislike that was especially intense among Western and Southern soldiers.

Yankees and Confederates alike developed a profound appreciation for solidarity. Most soldiers considered themselves independent individuals, but the extraordinary conditions of the war had created permanent bonds with other soldiers and barriers against noncombatants. In a veteran's eyes, there were men who knew what it was like to see a friend decapitated by a cannon shell or to march in the mud toward what could be one's own grave, and then there was the rest of the population who would never truly know any of this. Soldiers' bonds had helped to keep the armies together during the war, and they had the capacity to bring veterans together afterward.

But it would take extraordinary circumstances for a widespread revival of these bonds, and here the experience of Union and Confederate veterans diverged. Prominent Union veterans tried to translate wartime comradeship into peacetime organizations, but the GAR and other groups soon withered for lack of a compelling purpose. Southern attempts at organization did little better, but Southerners did find a cause that rekindled the solidarity of the war years. The Ku Klux Klan portrayed itself as the resurrected Confederate army, and post-Klan whites, completing their violent takeover of a

Southern state, employed all the trappings of a military campaign. The call to join old comrades against a perceived enemy made many veterans set aside their individualism and once again become part of a movement.

Union veterans found their cause, and their cause found them, in the 1880s. Eager politicians, a rejuvenated GAR, and the prospect of liberalized pensions all encouraged ex-Union soldiers to renew their old ties and act together. Although many Union veterans drifted away from organized activity afterward, those who remained were effective in ensuring a legacy of patriotic awareness among civilians.

Ex-Confederates' activism continued to follow a different course. They showed their own interest in formal organizations by the end of the 1880s, but this had little to do with pensions. The UCV did advocate expanded pensions and better-funded soldiers' homes, but these issues never approached the political appeal of Union pensions. The South rarely saw the kind of tight two-party competition in which pensions could provide the winning edge, and there was no single government to serve as the focus of Confederate pension lobbying. Confederate veterans played politics for different stakes—the racial functioning of their society.

Their significant role in beginning the movement to disfranchise African Americans was perhaps Confederate veterans' most conspicuous mark on Southern society. Ex-Confederates then turned to efforts that resembled Union veterans' campaigns to keep the war's memory alive and enforce public patriotism. This final parallel between Union and Confederate veterans' activities demonstrates the enduring power of the Civil War over its soldiers. All veterans had intensely personal memories of the war—revolting sights, frightening sounds, wrenching emotions, and countless other recollections—and they wanted people around them to acknowledge their special status. But to ensure this recognition they would have to act, as they had in the war, with their comrades. And so veterans joined secret groups and public organizations, went to the polls, spoke on Memorial Day, wrote to newspapers, and did whatever else they could to ensure they would not be forgotten.

Both sides accomplished some of the same things. Although the scale and nature of these accomplishments differed from North to South, each side made veterans' reunions noteworthy public events, each persuaded public officials to pay pensions and fund soldiers' homes, and each intervened in public education to pass on its version of the war. But Confederate veterans did this and more. Their vital role in subverting Republican governments and later in rewriting state constitutions went considerably beyond the feats of Union veterans. Civil War pensions, which brought Union veterans more attention than any other issue, had no direct connection with the few government pension plans that were enacted in the early twentieth century. Indeed, as Theda Skocpol points out, the main influence of Union pensions was to *delay* adoption of social insurance by public officials who were leery of uncontrolled social spending. Southerners' terrorism and constitutional changes, on the other hand, left a legacy of discrimination and segregation that would last until the civil-rights struggles of the mid-twentieth century.

Why did Confederate veterans have more influence than ex-Union soldiers? The heritage of defeat was certainly important: Confederate veterans' relentless pursuit of white supremacy was partly an atonement for losing the war. And Confederate veterans found themselves in situations where literal or symbolic militancy would produce tangible results. The Klan's activities and the subsequent intimidation of blacks mimicked army maneuvers, and agitators for disfranchisement often characterized their efforts as a paramilitary campaign. A Mississippi newspaper editor and former Confederate officer, for example, called on fellow Democrats in 1888 to "shake off your lethargy and show a little of the spirit of '75," when "the bonfires of the Democratic clans blazed from every hill top [and] the thunder of their campaign guns reverberated through every valley." Militant language and displays of military prowess came naturally to the Civil War generation, and old Confederates made the most of the chances they were given.

Union veterans, for their part, did not forget the martial spirit. Historians have noted in the late nineteenth century a resurgence of militarism that went well beyond the GAR's lobbying. Luminaries who were also Civil War veterans, such as jurist Oliver Wendell Holmes, Jr., and social scientist Francis Amasa Walker, increasingly characterized daily life as combat and expressed contempt for their society's softness and cowardice. But these men were restricted to speechmaking, however bellicose they might become; until the war with Spain, ex-Union soldiers lacked the opportunities that Southerners had to act on their concerns.

In truth, of course, the more than two million survivors of the Civil War had an enormous variety of ways to cope with their memories of the war. Some blotted it out, some vowed never to support another war, others romanticized everything about the conflict, and still others showed the long-term stress disorders that we associate with modern wars. What we have presented here were the most common attitudes and behavior of ex-soldiers.

To most veterans the Civil War was far more than an experience, because most experiences come to an end. Former soldiers believed that this war could not, and should not, end as long as its effects on combatants continued. Historians may not find fundamental character changes in Civil War soldiers, but veterans *believed* that the war had made them different from ordinary Americans, and that civilians did not appreciate the difference. Veterans had seen, as no one else had, the very best and worst that humans could do, and they feared this perception might die with them. Preventing the worst by promoting order and stability seemed to be their only course, and veterans conducted the crusade on a number of fronts—legislative halls, schools, parades, rural villages—with, as we have seen, varying success.

In so doing they set the stage for conservative activism by the veterans of twentieth-century wars. Historian William Pencak points out that the American Legion, which organized in the wake of World War I and took for itself the role of defining "Americanism," used the GAR as a model and established ties with the UCV. There was one legacy that Civil War veterans on both sides could claim equally: the insistence by the citizen-soldiers of each subsequent conflict that this was *their* war. This claim, originating in the deadliest of all American wars, will echo as long as wars produce survivors and memories.

A Note on Sources

MOBILIZING THE ARMIES

For a valuable overview of the changing American economy and its implications, see Bruce Laurie, *Artisans into Workers: Labor in Nineteenth-Century America* (New York, 1989). On the prevalence of the self-control ideal in the nineteenth century, see Daniel T. Rodgers, *The Work Ethic in Industrial America, 1850–1920* (Chicago, 1979), and Charles E. Rosenberg, "Sexuality, Class, and Role in 19th-Century America," *American Quarterly* 25 (1973), 131–153. For its institutional forms, see David Rothman, *The Discovery of the Asylum: Social Order and Disorder in the New Republic* (Boston, 1971). Carl N. Degler, *At Odds: Women and the Family in America from the Revolution to the Present* (New York, 1980), discusses child-rearing and self-control; on boyhood and masculinity, see E. Anthony Rotundo, *American Manhood: Transformations in Masculinity from the Revolution to the Modern Era* (New York, 1993). For evidence of nineteenth-century self-restraint, see Daniel Scott Smith and Michael S. Hindus, "Premarital Pregnancy in America, 1640–1971: An Overview and Interpretation," *Journal of Interdisciplinary History* 5 (1975), 537–570. Overviews of turnover in nineteenth-century communities are Donald H. Parkerson, "How Mobile Were Nineteenth-Century Americans?" *Historical Methods* 15 (1982), 99–110, and Richard H. Steckel, "Household Migration and Rural Settlement in the United States, 1850–1860," *Explorations in Economic History* 26 (1989), 190–218.

On war fever against Mexico, see Robert W. Johannsen, *To the Halls of the Montezumas: The Mexican War in the American Imagination* (New York, 1985). Marcus Cunliffe, *Soldiers and Civilians: The Martial Spirit in America, 1775–1865* (Boston, 1968), demonstrates antebellum apathy toward militia duty. The North's various mechanisms to raise troops are covered in James W. Geary, *We Need Men: The Union Draft in the Civil War* (DeKalb, Ill., 1991), and Eugene C. Murdock, *One Million Men: The Civil War Draft in the North* (Madison, Wisc., 1971). A careful study of draft evasion is Peter Levine, "Draft Evasion in the North During the Civil War," *Journal of American History* 67 (1981), 816–834.

The decision to recruit African-American troops is explained in Joseph T. Glatthaar, "Black Glory: The African-American Role in Union Victory," in Gabor S. Boritt, ed., *Why the Confederacy Lost* (New York, 1992), 135–162. The decision is also discussed, and numerous documents relating to black troops' experience are presented, in Ira Berlin, et al., eds., *The Black Military Experience,* Series II of *Freedom: A Documentary History of Emancipation* (Cambridge, Mass., 1982). Resistance to the draft is discussed in Phillip Shaw Paludan, *"A People's Contest": The Union and Civil War, 1861–1865* (New York, 1988), and the largest draft riot is examined in Iver Bernstein, *The New York City Draft Riots: Their Significance for American Society and Politics in the Age of the Civil War* (New York, 1990).

Essays on the war's demographic and social dimensions, and comparisons of Union soldiers with noncombatants, are included in the collection edited by Maris Vinovskis, *Toward a Social History of the American Civil War: Exploratory Essays* (New York, 1990). Another comparison of those who joined and those who did not is W. J. Rorabaugh, "Who Fought for the North in the Civil War? Concord, Massachusetts, Enlistments," *Journal of American History* 73 (1986), 695–701. William L. Barton, *Melting Pot Soldiers: The Union's Ethnic Regiments* (Ames, Iowa, 1988), describes recruitment of immigrants, and Kevin J. Weddle, "Ethnic Discrimination in Minnesota Volunteer Regiments During the Civil War," *Civil War History* 35 (1989), 239–259, cites prejudice in appointments and promotions. Charles Brewster's enlistment is examined in David W. Blight, "No Desperate Hero: Manhood and Freedom in a Union Soldier's Experience," in

Catherine Clinton and Nina Silber, eds., *Divided Houses: Gender and the Civil War* (New York, 1992), 55–75.

The events leading up to the outbreak of war, their context, and the course of the war itself are skillfully set out in James M. McPherson, *Battle Cry of Freedom: The Civil War Era* (New York, 1988). William W. Freehling offers intriguing reinterpretations of politics and the war's course in the essays collected in *The Reintegration of American History: Slavery and the Civil War* (New York, 1994), and includes a tour of the South in *The Road to Disunion: Secessionists at Bay, 1776–1854* (New York, 1990).

The issue of class relations in the antebellum South has generated too many studies to list here, but a good introduction and overview is Harry L. Watson, "Conflict and Collaboration: Yeomen, Slaveholders, and Politics in the Antebellum South," *Social History* 11 (1985), 273–298, and among more recent works, Bill Cecil-Fronsman, *Common Whites: Class and Culture in Antebellum North Carolina* (Lexington, Ky., 1992), is a particularly thorough examination. Bertram Wyatt-Brown, "Community, Class, and Snopesian Crime: Local Justice in the Old South," in Orville Vernon Burton and Robert C. McMath, Jr., eds., *Class, Conflict, and Consensus: Antebellum Southern Community Studies* (Westport, Conn., 1982), 173–206, explains the significance of Faulkner's "Barn Burning." Reid Mitchell, "The Creation of Confederate Loyalties," in Robert H. Abzug and Stephen E. Maizlish, eds., *New Perspectives on Race and Slavery in America: Essays in Honor of Kenneth M. Stampp* (Lexington, Ky., 1986), 93–108, and Paul D. Escott and Jeffrey J. Crow, "The Social Order and Violent Disorder: An Analysis of North Carolina in the Revolution and the Civil War," *Journal of Southern History* 52 (1986), 373–402, discuss class relations during the war. Vigilantism is examined in Michael Wayne, "An Old South Morality Play: Reconsidering the Social Underpinnings of the Proslavery Ideology," *Journal of American History* 77 (1990), 838–863: Winthrop D. Jordan, *Tumult and Silence at Second Creek: An Inquiry into a Civil War Slave Conspiracy* (Baton Rouge, 1993); and

Richard Maxwell Brown, *Strain of Violence: Historical Studies of American Violence and Vigilantism* (New York, 1975).

On Southern husbands' expectation of obedience from their wives, see Stephanie McCurry, "The Politics of Yeoman Households in South Carolina," in Clinton and Silber, *Divided Houses,* 22–38, and Joan E. Cashin, *A Family Venture: Men and Women on the Southern Frontier* (New York, 1991). The ties that united Southern communities are the focus of Robert C. Kenzer, *Kinship and Neighborhood in a Southern Community: Orange County, North Carolina, 1849–1881* (Knoxville, Tenn., 1987). On the centrality of honor in Southern male culture, see Bertram Wyatt-Brown, *Southern Honor: Ethics and Behavior in the Old South* (New York, 1982), and Edward L. Ayers, *Vengeance and Justice: Crime and Punishment in the 19th-Century American South* (New York, 1984).

William L. Barney, *The Secessionist Impulse: Alabama and Mississippi in 1860* (Princeton, N.J., 1974), includes a good discussion of the treatment of Unionists. Albert B. Moore, *Conscription and Conflict in the Confederacy* (New York, 1924), remains the only full-length study of the Southern draft. The most extensive comparison of reasons for Union and Confederate soldiers' enlistment is James M. McPherson, *What They Fought For: 1861–1865* (Baton Rouge, 1994). A smaller study of soldiers' letters and diaries is Pete Maslowski, "A Study of Morale in Civil War Soldiers," *Military Affairs* 34 (1970), 122–126. Michael Barton, *Goodmen: The Character of Civil War Soldiers* (University Park, Pa., 1981), carefully applies the techniques of content analysis to soldiers' testimony.

For a comparison of Confederate soldiers and noncombatants see Larry M. Logue, "Who Joined the Confederate Army? Soldiers, Civilians, and Communities in Mississippi," *Journal of Social History* 26 (1993) 611–623; J. William Harris, *Plain Folk and Gentry in a Slave Society: White Liberty and Black Slavery in Augusta's Hinterlands* (Middletown, Conn., 1985), reaches a different conclusion on the background of volunteers but uses more limited evidence on enlistment. Comparisons of Confederate and Union enlistees are Peter Wallenstein, "Which Side Are You On? The Social Origins of White Union Troops from Civil War Tennessee," *Journal of East Tennessee History* 63 (1991), 72–103, and Wayne K. Durrill, *War of Another Kind: A Southern Community in the Great Rebellion* (New York, 1990). Martin Crawford, "Confederate Volunteering and Enlistment in Ashe County, North Carolina, 1861–1862," *Civil War History* 37 (1991), 29–50, discusses the role of the community in raising troops. The Confederate government's attempts to prevent unauthorized travel are described in Kenneth Radley, *Rebel Watchdog: The Confederate States Army Provost Guard* (Baton Rouge, 1989).

SOLDIERS AT WAR

The prevailing American attitude toward death is discussed in Lewis O. Saum, *The Popular Mood of Pre-Civil War America* (Westport, Conn., 1980). The pioneering study of life in the Union army is Bell Irvin Wiley, *The Life of Billy Yank* (Indianapolis, 1952). Most of the more recent studies of Civil War soldiers include men on both sides. Those that devote the most attention to interpretation and analysis are Gerald Linderman, *Embattled Courage: The Experience of Combat in the American Civil War* (New York, 1987), and Reid Mitchell, *Civil War Soldiers: Their Expectations and Their Experiences* (New York, 1988). Other studies that focus more on description include Randall C. Jimerson, *The Private Civil War: Popular Thought During the Sectional Conflict* (Baton Rouge, 1988); Joseph Allan Frank and George A. Reaves, *"Seeing the Elephant": Raw Recruits at the Battle of Shiloh* (Westport, Conn., 1989); and James I. Robertson, Jr., *Soldiers Blue and Gray* (Columbia, S.C., 1988). Studies that concentrate on Union soldiers include Reid Mitchell, *The Vacant Chair: The Northern Soldier Leaves Home* (New York, 1993), and Joseph T. Glatthaar, *The March to the Sea and Beyond: Sherman's Troops in the Savannah and Carolinas Campaigns* (New York, 1986).

A provocative revision of accepted wisdom on Civil War weapons and tactics is Paddy Griffith, *Battle Tactics of the Civil War* (New Haven, Conn., 1989). For studies that assign religion a somewhat greater role in the Union army than does the Linderman analysis, see Gardiner H. Shattuck, Jr., *A Shield and Hiding Place: The Religious Life of the Civil War Armies* (Macon, Ga., 1987), and Gregory J. W. Urwin, "'The Lord Has Not Forsaken Me and I Won't Forsake Him': Religion in Frederick Steele's Union Army, 1863–1864," *Arkansas Historical Quarterly* 52 (1993), 318–340. On Union chaplains, see Richard M. Budd, "Ohio Army Chaplains and the Professionalization of Military Chaplaincy in the Civil War," *Ohio History* 102 (1993), 5–19.

The wartime experience of black soldiers is detailed in Joseph T. Glatthaar, *Forged in Battle: The Civil War Alliance of Black Soldiers and White Officers* (New York, 1990). Civil War medical practice is surveyed in Stewart Brooks, *Civil War Medicine* (Springfield, Ill., 1966), and Paul E. Steiner, *Disease in the Civil War* (Springfield, Ill., 1968); the experience of nurses on both sides is explored in Jane E. Schultz, "The Inhospitable Hospital: Gender and Professionalism in Civil War Medicine," *Signs* 17 (1992), 363–392. Medical care in the Union army is detailed in George W. Adams, *Doctors in Blue: The Medical History of the Union Army in the Civil War* (New York, 1952). An insightful examination of the United States Sanitary Commission appears in George M. Fredrickson, *The Inner Civil War: Northern Intellectuals and the Crisis of the Union* (New York, 1965).

The best study of Union soldiers as prisoners of war is William Marvel, *Andersonville: The Last Depot* (Chapel Hill, 1994). On combat stress, see Eric T. Dean, Jr., "'We Will All Be Lost and Destroyed': Post-Traumatic Stress Disorder and the Civil War," *Civil War History* 37 (1991), 138–153. Judith Lee Hallock, "The Role of the Community in Civil War Desertion," *Civil War History* 29 (1983), 123–134, compares cohesive and unsettled townships. Guerrilla warfare is thoroughly examined in

Michael Fellman, *Inside War: The Guerrilla Conflict in Missouri During the American Civil War* (New York, 1989).

Bell Irvin Wiley also pioneered the study of Confederate soldiers with *The Life of Johnny Reb* (Indianapolis, 1943). On life in specific armies, see Bob Womack, *Call Forth the Mighty Men* (Bessemer, Ala., 1987), and Larry J. Daniel, *Soldiering in the Army of Tennessee: A Portrait of Life in a Confederate Army* (Chapel Hill, 1991). The Celtic influence on Southern tactics is argued in Grady McWhiney and Perry D. Jamieson, *Attack and Die: Civil War Military Tactics and the Southern Heritage* (University, Ala., 1982), and disputed in Richard E. Beringer, et al., *Why the South Lost the Civil War* (Athens, Ga., 1986).

Confederate medical practice is examined in Horace H. Cunningham, *Doctors in Gray: The Confederate Medical Service* (Baton Rouge, 1958). Analyses of Confederates as prisoners are scarce; among the more careful efforts is James I. Robertson, Jr., "The Scourge of Elmira," *Civil War History* 8 (1962), 184–201. Complements to the Fellman study that expand on guerrillas and the Confederacy are Phillip Shaw Paludan, *Victims: A True Story of the Civil War* (Knoxville, Tenn., 1981), and Daniel G. Sutherland, "Guerrillas: The Real War in Arkansas," *Arkansas Historical Quarterly* 52 (1993), 257–285. In addition to the Shattuck study cited above, two articles examine religious enthusiasm among Confederates: Drew Gilpin Faust, "Christian Soldiers: The Meaning of Revivalism in the Confederate Army," *Journal of Southern History* 53 (1987), 63–90, and Samuel J. Watson, "Religion and Combat Motivation in the Confederate Armies," *Journal of Military History* 58 (1994), 29–55.

Analyses of Confederate desertion include Richard Reid, "A Test Case of the 'Crying Evil': Desertion Among North Carolina Troops During the Civil War," *North Carolina Historical Review* 58 (1981), 234–262; Bessie Martin, *Desertion of Alabama Troops from the Confederate Army: A Study in Sectionalism* (New York, 1966); and Victoria Bynum, *Unruly Women: The Politics of Social and Sexual Control in the Old South* (Chapel Hill, N.C., 1992). For two very different views of desertion from specific units, see Kevin C. Ruffner, "Civil War Desertion from a Black Belt Regiment: An Examination of the 44th Virginia Infantry," in Edward L. Ayers and John C. Wills, eds., *The Edge of the South: Life in Nineteenth-Century Virginia* (Charlottesville, Va., 1991), 79–108, and Robert K. Krick, "The Army of Northern Virginia in September of 1862," in Gary W. Gallagher, ed., *Antietam: Essays on the 1862 Maryland Campaign* (Kent, Ohio, 1989), 35–55.

CIVIL WAR VETERANS AND POSTWAR AMERICA

The essential source for understanding the immediate postwar years is Eric Foner, *Reconstruction: America's Unfinished Revolution, 1863–1877* (New York, 1988). A dated but thorough account of soldiers' return is Dixon Wecter, *When Johnny Comes Marching Home* (Boston, 1944). Glatthaar, *Forged in Battle,* includes a discussion of blacks' postwar experience, and Kevin R. Hardwick, "'Your Old Father Abe Lincoln Is Dead and Damned': Black Soldiers and the Memphis Race Riot of 1866," *Journal of Social History* 27 (1993), 109–128, illustrates whites' resentment. Stuart McConnell, *Glorious Contentment: The Grand Army of the Republic, 1865–1900* (Chapel Hill, 1992), analyzes the organizing impulse among Union veterans; Mary R. Dearing, *Veterans in Politics: The Story of the G.A.R.* (Baton Rouge, 1952), and Wallace E. Davies, *Patriotism on Parade: The Story of Veterans' and Hereditary Organizations in America, 1783–1900* (Cambridge, Mass., 1955), trace veterans' political activity.

The best assessment of postwar crime rates is in Eric H. Monkkonen, *Police in Urban America, 1860–1920* (New York, 1981). On drug addiction among Union veterans, see David Courtwright, "Opiate Addiction as a Consequence of the Civil War," *Civil War History* 24 (1978), 101–111. Rhode Island data are from unpublished research by the present author. The standard legislative history of Union pensions is William H. Glasson, *Federal Military Pensions in the United States* (New York, 1918), and the standard account of soldiers' homes is Judith G. Cetina, "A History of Veterans' Homes in the United States: 1811–1930" (Ph.D. dissertation, Case Western Reserve University, 1977). Larry M. Logue, "Union Veterans and Their Government: The Effects of Public Policies on Private Lives," *Journal of Interdisciplinary History* 22 (1992), 411–434, assesses the social effects of pensions and soldiers' homes. On pension applications and party politics, see Heywood T. Sanders, "Paying for the 'Bloody Shirt': The Politics of Civil War Pensions," in Barry S. Rundquist, ed., *Political Benefits: Empirical Studies of American Public Programs* (Lexington, Mass., 1980), 137–159.

Confederate soldiers' attitudes are traced in Michael Barton, "Did the Confederacy Change Southern Soldiers? Some Obvious and Some Unobtrusive Measures," in Harry P. Owens and James J. Cooke, eds., *The Old South in the Crucible of War* (Jackson, Miss., 1983), 65–79. On postwar violence, see Dan T. Carter, *When the War Was Over: The Failure of Self-Reconstruction in the South, 1865–1867* (Baton Rouge, 1985). Gaines M. Foster, *Ghosts of the Confederacy: Defeat, the Lost Cause, and the Emergence of the New South, 1865 to 1913* (New York, 1987), examines veterans' responses to defeat and their organizing tendencies, and Charles Reagan Wilson, *Baptized in Blood: The Religion of the Lost Cause, 1865–1920* (Athens, Ga., 1980), focuses on those who were determined to ennoble the Confederate cause. Mississippi election data are from unpublished research by the present author. For Alabama marriage rates, see Robert A. Gilmour, "The Other Emancipation: Studies in the Society and Economy of Alabama Whites During Reconstruction," (Ph.D. dissertation, Johns Hopkins University, 1972).

The standard history of the Reconstruction-era Ku Klux Klan is Allen W. Trelease, *White Terror: The Ku Klux Klan Conspiracy and Southern Reconstruction* (New York, 1971). On the Klan's attacks and related violence in the period, see George C. Rable, *But There Was No Peace: The Role of Violence in the Politics of Reconstruction* (Athens, Ga., 1984). The Klan's roots are explored in

Gladys-Marie Fry, *Night Riders in Black Folk History* (Knoxville, Tenn., 1975); Bertram Wyatt-Brown, *Honor and Violence in the Old South* (New York, 1986); Charles L. Flynn, Jr., "The Ancient Pedigree of Violent Repression: Georgia's Klan as a Folk Movement," in Walter J. Fraser, Jr., and Winfred B. Moore, Jr., eds., *The Southern Enigma: Essays on Race, Class, and Folk Culture* (Westport, Conn., 1983), 189–198; and William D. Piersen, "Family Secrets: How African-American Culture Shaped the Early Ku Klux Klan," in Winfred B. Moore, Jr., and Joseph F. Tripp, eds., *Looking South: Chapters in the Story of an American Region* (Westport, Conn., 1989), 41–50. Wartime and postwar Southern resistance are contrasted in Kenneth M. Stampp, *The Imperiled Union: Essays on the Background of the Civil War* (New York, 1980).

The epilogue to Linderman, *Embattled Courage,* traces the ebb and flow of late-nineteenth-century interest in the war, and Mark C. Carnes, *Secret Ritual and Manhood in Victorian America* (New Haven, Conn., 1989), examines secret societies. The best and most comprehensive study of the New South, including its agrarian political movements and race relations, is Edward L. Ayers, *The Promise of the New South: Life After Reconstruction* (New York, 1992). As yet there is no detailed study of Confederate pensions; the best place to follow their progress is in the pages of *Confederate Veteran,* a monthly magazine that began publication in 1893. James R. Young, "Confederate Pensions in Georgia, 1886–1929," *Georgia Historical Quarterly* 66 (1982), 47–52, notes the proportion of state budgets consumed by pensions. R. B. Rosenburg, *Living Monuments: Confederate Soldiers' Homes in the New South* (Chapel Hill, 1993), examines the homes and their residents.

An intriguing account of aging Confederates' concern for their legacy is David Herbert Donald, "A Generation of Defeat," in Walter J. Fraser, Jr., and Winfred B. Moore, Jr., eds., *From the Old South to the New: Essays on the Transitional South* (Westport, Conn., 1981), 3–20. The best study of the disfranchising conventions is J. Morgan Kousser, *The Shaping of Southern Politics: Suf-*

frage Restriction and the Establishment of the One-Party South, 1880–1910 (New Haven, Conn., 1974). Data on convention elections in Mississippi and South Carolina are from unpublished research by the author.

Theda Skocpol, *Protecting Soldiers and Mothers: The Political Origins of Social Policy in the United States* (Cambridge, Mass., 1992), discusses the nature and consequences of Civil War pensions. William Graebner, *A History of Retirement: The Meaning and Function of an American Institution, 1885–1978* (New Haven, Conn., 1980), and Carole Haber, *Beyond Sixty-Five: The Dilemma of Old Age in America's Past* (New York, 1983), explain changes in the concept of retirement. Data on the Missouri Confederate soldiers' home are from unpublished research by the present author. Information on the last survivors of the war (on both sides) appears in Jay S. Hoar, *The South's Last Boys in Gray* (Bowling Green, Ohio, 1986). Clyde Griffen raises intriguing questions about the war's long-term effects on Northerners' attitudes in "Reconstructing Masculinity from the Evangelical Revival to the Waning of Progressivism: A Synthesis," in Mark C. Carnes and Clyde Griffen, eds., *Meanings for Manhood: Constructions of Masculinity in Victorian America* (Chicago, 1990), 183–204. William Pencak, *For God and Country: The American Legion, 1919–1941* (Boston, 1989), traces the influence of Civil War veterans' groups on the Legion.

Index

A NOTE ON THE AUTHOR

Larry M. Logue teaches American history at Mississippi College in Clinton, Mississippi. He received a B.A. from the University of Pittsburgh and a Ph.D. in American civilization from the University of Pennsylvania, and has written frequently on aspects of American social history. His book *A Sermon in the Desert: Belief and Behavior in Early St. George, Utah,* was awarded the Chipman Prize by the Mormon History Association.